"In the Name of Allāh, the Most Beneficent,
the Most Merciful"

Contents

Introduction … … … … … … … … … … … … … … … … ...	6
Fireworks … … … … … … … … … … … … … … … … …	8
3 Pieces of Advice Versus 20 Years of Salary … … … ... … … .	9
Shaykh Maulānā Islāmul Haq Sāhib ﷺ … … … … … … …	13
Unity … … … … … … … … … … … … … … … … … …	14
Different Categories of Muslim … … … … … … … … … …	17
Importance of Madrasah … … … … … … … … … … … … .	20
The Madrasah System - The Pride of our Community … … …	21
Amazing Advice by the Great Scholar Imām Ibnul Qayyim ﷺ ...	24
Never be Rude and Arrogant to Anyone … … … … … … … .	25
Colonel Amiruddin Sāhib ﷺ … … … … … … … … … …	26
Advice to the Scholars … … … … … … … … … … … … ..	29
Everybody has a Different Story … … … … … … … … … .	31
Imagine … … … … … … … … … … … … … … … … … .	32
Most Hated … … … … … … … … … … … … … … … …	34
Ahlul– Bayt … … … … … … … … … … … … … … … …	35
I'tikāf … … … … … … … … … … … … … … … … …	36
Values … … … … … … … … … … … … … … … … … …	40
Solidarity with Refugees … … … … … … … … … … … …	41
The Fly and Antibiotics … … … … … … … … … … … … ..	43
Message for Muslims in the West … … … … … … … … …	45
I Hear the Salām of a Zā'ir (Visitor) at My Grave … … … … ..	50
Sayyidunā Uthmān ﷺ … … … … … … … … … … … …	54
A Perfect Poem, Written in the Saddest Way … … … … … …	56

The Best Season for the Believer… … … … … … … … … … …...	**59**
Fasting on the 10th of Muharram… … … … … … … … … … ….	**60**
Spending on the Day of Āshoorā … … … … … … … … … ….	**61**
Incidents During Muharram… … … … … … … … … … …..…	**63**
True Love… … … … … …...… … … … … … … … … … … …	**64**
The Last Day the Prophet ﷺ Smiled...… … … … … … … …	**66**
Sūfism … … … … … …..… … … … … … … … … … … … …..	**69**
Memory of the Beloved Prophet ﷺ … … … … … … … … …	**73**
5 Ways to Make your Child Love to Pray… … … … … … …..	**79**
Rise Among the Elite … … … … … … … … … … … … … …...	**86**
The Woman Who was Given the Title 'The Martyr' Whilst She was Living!..	**88**
A Glimpse into the Nurturing of Maulānā As'ad Madani ؓ of his Daughter...… … … … … … … … … … … … … … … …	**92**

Introduction

All praises are due to Allāh ﷻ and may peace and salutations be upon the Last of the Messengers, our Beloved Prophet Muhammad ﷺ, upon his honourable Companions ؓ and upon those who follow their virtuous lifestyles until the final hour.

This book contains a selection of articles which have been gathered for the benefit of the readers covering a variety of topics on various aspects of daily life. It offers precious advice and anecdotes that contain moral lessons. The advice will captivate its readers and will extend the narrowness of their thoughts to deep reflection, wisdom and appreciation of the purpose of our existence.

The objective of this book is to present different types of beneficial advice so that we can implement them into our daily lives. Mulla Nasr-ud-Deen, famously known for his wittiness and smartness, was once asked about what he considered the most precious thing in the world. His response was that advice is the most priceless thing. Yet on another occasion he was asked what was the most worthless thing in the world and his response was also advice. In removing the contradiction of his statement he eloquently said, *"An advice taken may be priceless, but consider how worthless it becomes when it is not taken."*

This book contains special advice and tips about life in general. It also includes life experiences which the readers can relate to. As

Mullah Nasr-ud-Deen rightly said that these precious advices become beneficial and priceless only when they are taken seriously.

May Allāh ﷻ accept this compilation, benefit us from the precious advices contained in this book and reward my beloved teacher and Shaykh, Mufti Saiful Islām Sāhib in the life of this world and the Hereafter for his efforts. Āmeen!

Maulāna Ismāeel Aziz
Graduate of JKN
October 2016/ Muharram 1439

Fireworks

Hakeemul-Ummah Shaykh Ashraf Ali Thānwi ﷺ has written in his famous work Behishti Zewar (Heavenly Ornaments), that participating in fireworks would not be permissible for a few reasons:

1) Wastage of money of which Allāh ﷻ says:

"Give due right to the close relatives, the poor and the travellers. Do not be extravagant, surely the extravagant ones are the friends of Shaytān, and Shaytān has always been ungrateful to his Lord." (17:26-27)

Note: Some Arab countries spend millions of pounds to have the biggest fireworks display ever to enter the Guinness Book of Records. This is while their Muslims neighbours are dying of hunger in Syria and Palestine.

Give Sadaqah and protect yourself from the fire of Jahannam. If you happen to pass by a Bonfire, think that if this is so hot, how will the heat of Jahannam be?

2) Dangerous
Accident & emergency wards get extremely busy on such occasions. Many cases of death and severe injuries by fireworks are recorded worldwide. Fire departments are also on high alert. In some coun-

tries, tyres are burnt and roads are damaged, requiring expensive sums for repair. Then there is the pollution, the noise etc.

3) Immoral activities
Many a times it involves intermingling of the sexes which leads to immoral activities in the darkness of the night. Some teenagers from good backgrounds also start behaving in that manner. As they say 'kharbooza kharbooza se rang pakarta he' i.e. a melon catches the colour of the one next to it'

3 Pieces of Advice Versus 20 Years of Salary

A very poor newly wedded, young couple lived in a small farm. One day, the husband made the following proposal to his wife: Honey, I will leave the house. I will travel faraway, get a job and work hard in order to come back and give you the comfortable life that you deserve. I do not know how long I will stay away, I only ask one thing, please wait for me and while I am away, you should be faithful to me, because I will be faithful to you.

So the young man left. He walked many days until he found a farmer who was in need of someone to help him. The young man offered his services. He was accepted and therefore, he discussed the terms with his boss: Let me work for as long as I want and when I think I should go home, please relieve me of my duties. I do not want to receive my salary. I ask you to save it for me until the day I leave. The day I decide to go, please give me the money and I will go my way. They agreed on that.

So, the young man worked for twenty years without holiday and without rest. After twenty years, he came to his boss and said: Boss, I want my money, because I am returning to my home.

The boss replied: All right, after all, I made a deal with you and I will stick to it. However, before you go, I want to offer you something new: I will give you all your money and send you away; or I will give you 3 pieces of advice and send you away. If I give you the money, I will not give you the 3 pieces of advice and if I give you the 3 pieces of advice, I will not give you the money. Now, go to your room and think about your answer.

He thought for two days. Then he went to the boss and told him: I want the 3 pieces of advice. The boss stressed again: If I give you the 3 pieces of advice, I will not give you the money. The man replied: I want the 3 pieces of advice.

The boss then told him: No. 1: Never take shortcuts in your life; shorter and unknown paths can cost your life. No. 2: Never be too curious, for curiosity towards evil can be deadly. No. 3: Never make decisions in moments of anger or pain, because when you repent, it could be too late.

After giving these 3 pieces of advice, the boss said to him: Here, you have 3 loaves of bread, 2 are for you to eat during the journey and the last is for you to eat with your wife when you get home. So the man went his way, after twenty years away from home and from his wife, whom he loved so much.

After the first day of travel, he found a man who greeted him and asked: Where are you going? He replied: To a distant place which is about 20 days away if I continue walking. The man said to him: O' man, this path is too long! I know a shortcut that is very safe and you will arrive in 5 days only.

The man began to follow the path suggested until he remembered the first piece of advice. Then, he returned and followed the long path. Days later, he learned that the shortcut led to an ambush.

After a few more days of travel, he found an inn by the roadside, where he could rest. He paid for a room and after taking a bath, he lay down to sleep. During the night, he woke up as he heard a terrifying scream. He rose to his feet and went to the door to check what happened. As he was opening the door, he remembered the second piece of advice. Therefore he returned, lay down again and slept.

At dawn, after breakfast, the owner of the lodging asked him if he had not heard the scream at night. He affirmed that he heard. Then the host said: Were you not curious to see what happened? He replied: No, I was not. Then the host said: You are the first guest to leave this inn alive. My neighbour is completely crazy. He usually shouts at night to call someone's attention. When some of the guests come out, he kills them and buries their bodies in the backyard.

The man continued his long journey, eager to arrive soon. After many days and nights walking, he was very tired, but he finally saw his house far away. It was night. He saw some light coming out of the window of his house and was able to see the silhouette of his wife. However, he also saw that she was not alone. He came closer and saw that there was a man with her. She softly caressed his hair.

When he saw that scene, his heart was filled with hatred and bitterness. He decided to rush and kill them both mercilessly. However, he took a deep breath and he remembered the third piece of advice. Then he stopped, reflected and decided to sleep outside that night. He slept in the midst of the bushes, determined to make a decision the next day.

At dawn, he was calmer and thought: I will not kill my wife and her lover. I am going back to my boss to ask him to take me back but before I go, I want to tell my wife that I have always been faithful to her. He went to the front door and knocked. When his wife opened the door and recognized him, she cried and embraced him warmly. He tried to push her away, but he was not able to do so. Then, with tears in his eyes he told her: I was faithful to you but you betrayed me.

She was shocked, so she replied: How did I betray you? I have never betrayed you. I waited patiently for you for twenty good years. Then he asked: How about the man that you were caressing yesterday? She said: That man is your son. When you left, I discovered I was pregnant. Today he is twenty years old.

Hearing that, the man asked for her forgiveness. He met and hugged his son. Then he told them all the things he had experienced while away. Meanwhile, his wife prepared some coffee for them to have together with the last bread given by his boss.

After a prayer of thanksgiving, he broke the bread. When he looked at it, he found all his money inside. In fact, there was even more than the right payment for his twenty years of dedication and hard work.

Our Creator is like this boss. When he asks us to make a sacrifice, he wants to give us more than what we give Him. He wants us to have His unique wisdom as well as the material blessings.

Shaykh Islāmul Haq Sāhib ؒ

Shaykh Muhammad Saleem Dhorat Sāhib said that when Shaykh Islāmul Haq Sāhib ؒ first came to England, even though he was so busy in teaching Ahādeeth books etc, (1) He never missed Takbeer Oola (the first Takbeer of Salāh) (2) He would recite one Manzil of the Qur'ān daily even though he was not a Hāfiz. (3) You would never hear Gheebat in any of his Majlis (gathering).

Unity

Shaykh Mufti Rafee' Uthmāni Sāhib speaking about creating unity within the Ummah, recited the famous verses of Sūrah Āl-Imrān,

$$\text{يَا أَيُّهَا الَّذِيْنَ آمَنُوا اتَّقُوا اللهَ حَقَّ تُقَاتِهِ وَلَا تَمُوْتُنَّ إِلَّا وَأَنْتُمْ مُسْلِمُوْنَ}$$
$$\text{وَاعْتَصِمُوْا بِحَبْلِ اللهِ جَمِيْعًا وَّلَا تَفَرَّقُوْا}$$

"O Believers! Fear Allāh as He deserves to be feared and do not die except as Muslims. Hold fast to the rope of Allāh altogether and do not be divided into groups."(3:102)

He said ponder over the words "Wa Lā Tafarraqu"(Do not divide). It is not "Wa Lā Takhtalifu" (Do not differ). This implies that we can have differences but we shouldn't be divided into Firqas (group) and sects. Difference of opinions is in all fields. It is a sign of people's intelligence. However, wise people do not argue among themselves. They may differ but they respect one another.

Allāh ﷻ gave us the name 'Muslims'. We should stick to that name and avoid sectarianism.

Our beloved Prophet ﷺ hated causing disputes. One Hadeeth of Bukhāri states that He wished he could reconstruct the Ka'bah upon the foundations laid by Sayyidunā Ibrāheem ﷺ. However, he said this would cause a confusion among the community, so he left it as it was.

Shaykh Mufti Rafee' Uthmāni Sāhib quoted the Hadeeth of Sayyidunā Abū Saeed Khudri ؓ, who came to perform Eid Salāh with the governor of Madeenah Munawwarah, Marwān Ibn Hakam. Marwān had a pulpit set out for him and went towards it to deliver the Khutbah. Sayyidunā Abū Saeed ؓ pulled his hand towards the Musalla (prayer mat) and said "Salāh is performed first in Eid, while the Khutbah comes after it." However, Marwān insisted and went for the Khutbah. Another person also objected but Marwān did not listen.

Sayyidunā Abū Saeed ؓ said, "This person has done his job. I heard Rasūlullāh ﷺ say, "Whoever sees a Munkar (wrong), should correct it with his hands; if he cannot, then with his tongue; if he cannot then with his heart." (i.e. he should realise that this is wrong though I am not in a position to change it).

Mufti Rafee' Sāhib said, "Sayyidunā Abū Saeed ؓ could have easily gone to another side and started his own Eid Salāh and most people would have definitely followed him but that would have caused a split among the people; so he just went along with what Marwān was doing.

He said, "For changing a Munkar (wrong doing), first we need to have proper knowledge of that Munkar, then we should be moderate in our approach. Today, we have arguments and disputes in the Masjid and we fight over trivial matters. We call one another names. We cannot come to agree on anything. This is a very sad state of the Ummah.

I have come to the UK on many occasions. Alhamdulillāh, on the bright side, we see the increase in Masājid and Madāris (Islamic Schools). We get a lot of hope from this. However, at the same time, the deep division between communities is also increasing. We in Pakistan have a great deal of chaos. You should protect yourselves by agreeing to disagree and acknowledging the differences but respecting one another."

He went on to give some examples from Fuqahā for avoiding disunity. He said, "If the Imām makes a major mistake in Eid Salāh, he is not obliged to do Sajdah Sahw. This is because the gathering is huge and Sajdah Sahw will cause a confusion among the crowd. People might not understand, their Salāh will be at risk and they could start arguing after the Salāh.

Further, performing Janāzah Salāh in the Masjid is Makrooh Tahreemi, but Fuqahā have said that if by praying it outside the Masjid, we might be obstructing those who are passing by, then we should pray it inside the Masjid. How long does Janāzah Salāh take? Only a few minutes, but even that slightest inconvenience of others is not tolerated.

So we should try to make peace with everyone and live with harmony. "

During the final Du'ā he repeated these words a few times,

اَللّٰهُمَّ اَلِّفْ بَيْنَ قُلُوْبِنَا وَ أَصْلِحْ ذَاتَ بَيْنِنَا وَاهْدِنَا سُبُلَ السَّلَامِ

"O' Allāh! Create love within our hearts and make good our relations and guide us along the paths of peace."

Different Categories of Muslim

In these sensitive times for Muslims, this is how we will see the Muslims split up:

1) The first group will talk and write a lot without doing anything, neither to better their Deen or to better the world we live in. These people are useless. They feel sorry for themselves and spend too much time on social media and the news but have no time to raise their hands and ask from Allāh ﷻ, nor pray a few Rak'ats and pledge to do something positive for the world.

2) The second group will start online petitions etc, and will make a commendable effort for the world, but will give no importance to their Deen. These are better than the first, but have work to do. They need to reconnect fully with Allāh ﷻ and realise that Allāh ﷻ holds the keys to all of our problems.

3) The third group are the people who realise the problem is from within. The problem is not Islām. The problem is a lack of Islām in our hearts. If we are true Muslims and do what is demanded of us, we would never be in these problems.

These are the people who read the Qur'ān and realise that Allāh ﷻ says: **"If you help Allāh (His religion), He will help you and keep your feet firm." (47:7)** Allāh ﷻ also says: **"If Allāh helps you, nobody will be able to overwhelm you."(3:160)**

These people realise the solution is to become better Muslims and better people. These people help others come to the Deen and start practicing properly. These people spend their free time crying to Allāh ﷻ for humanity.

These people have read the Ahādeeth wherein the Messenger ﷺ said, "If you stop calling to the good and you stop preventing the evil, a time will come when you will ask from Allāh ﷻ and He will not give, you will pray to Him and He will not respond, He will give people power over you who will have no mercy on you, He will turn you against each other."

4) The fourth group of people are the best. They do everything like the people in group 3 and they help the world they live in. These people will make resolutions to better themselves and the society they live in.

The prescribed method from Allāh ﷻ and His beloved Messenger ﷺ to get ourselves out of this problem, is to turn back to Allāh ﷻ and help others turn back to Allāh ﷻ. When the Masjid is full for Fajr as it is for Jumu'ah, we will see the changes in the world that Allāh ﷻ will bring. Problems will be alleviated by Allāh ﷻ and His mercy will descend.

Continue doing Istighfār (asking for forgiveness) and ask Allāh ﷻ to overlook our faults and to spare us from punishment in both worlds although we are deserving of it.

Recite this Du'ā abundantly for the Ummah:

$$\text{لَا إِلَهَ إِلَّا أَنْتَ سُبْحَانَكَ إِنِّيْ كُنْتُ مِنَ الظَّالِمِيْنَ}$$

May Allāh ﷻ make us from the third and the fourth group, and enable us to make resolutions about our future; to fulfil our religious and social obligations, to spend time asking from Allāh ﷻ, to shed a tear for humanity and to become better Muslims and better humans. Āmeen!

Importance of Madrasah

Why do we always differentiate between school and Madrasah ?

We send our kids to school as early as 3 years, yet we think they are too young for Madrasah.

We send them to the most expensive schools, yet we send them to our local Masjid for Madrasah.

We always get a part time teacher if they have problems at school, yet we do not do the same for Madrasah.

We enrol them in summer classes, yet we do not do the same for Madrasah.

We encourage our kids to practice what they are learning at school, yet we do not do the same for Madrasah.

We go an extra mile to make sure our kids have done their homework, yet we do not even ask what they studied in Madrasah.

We scold our kids when they do not attend school, yet a day or two of missing Madrasah is nothing wrong.

We promise our kids gifts if they get a good position at school, yet we cannot even promise anything for Madrasah.

We tell the whole world how our children have performed at school, yet we cannot even tell our friends when our child has finished Juzz Amma (30th Part of the Qur'ān).

While young, children grow up knowing how less important Madrasah is in their life. They cannot even equate it to school and it's all because we as parents show them its less important. Let's show our children that Madrasah is as equally important as the School.

*A Maktab (Madrasah) has stood the test of time. Nothing can replace it.

The Madrasah System - The Pride of Our Community

The Christian community has the Church, the Jewish community has its Synagogue, the Hindu Community has its Mandir, the Sikh community has the Gurdwara and the Buddhists have their Temple and so on…..But the Muslim community not only has the Masjid but also the educational institute - Madrasah.

Alhamdulillāh, Allāh ﷻ has blessed the Muslims with such a great bounty where children from as young as five learn to read the Qur'ān, Islamic Tāreekh (history), Ādāb & Akhlāq (Manners and Etiquettes), Hadeeth (Traditions of the Holy Prophet ﷺ), Fiqh (Basic Islamic Rulings) and much more. This is also where children complete Hifz (the memorisation of 30 chapters, 114 Sūrah's and over 6000 verses of the Holy Qur'ān!).

This in itself is a miracle of Allāh ﷻ, but the message intended by this is that the Madrasah system is a bounty which through the efforts of our pious predecessors, for hundreds of years, has educated us and has saved many of us from becoming completely neglectful of the Deen.

How many Jews can read the Torah in its original Hebrew text? How many Christians can read the Bible in its original Aramaic text? How many Sikhs and Hindus can read their respective books in their original text?

Today, more than 80% of Muslims can read the Holy Qur'ān in its original Arabic text. This is all through the blessings of the Madrasah which even your local 'Molvi' (scholar) owes a great deal to. Through the Madrasah, an individual bases his or her moral values which carries them throughout their life.

Unfortunately nowadays, we do not value the Madrasah as much as our predecessors did. Islamic education is being disregarded. Instead of sending our children to the Madrasah to gain the necessary Islamic knowledge and practice, we prefer sending them to an after-school homework club or to football practice. We have this attitude and tend to think that when our son or daughter has completed the recitation of the Holy Qur'ān once or twice, then their Islamic education is complete. We do not fully realise the spiritual benefit of the Madrasah.

As soon as a child steps out of the house, he or she becomes exposed to various kinds of outside evil temptations and mischief. The child falls prey to the tricks of the Shaytān. As soon as they enter environments where there is little respect of teachers and the child sees the area as unsanctified, flirtation becomes a norm, swearing becomes a core part of the limited vocabulary, slander and backbiting become the discussions of the day. So many other vices become part of the child's everyday life.

However, when a child comes home, performs Wudhu and then goes to the Madrasah, he/she will be safeguarded from these satanic practices. The child will sit in such an environment where the words of Allāh ﷻ are recited in melodious tunes, stories of the Ambiyā (Prophets) ﷺ are mentioned and Sunnats are explained. What can be a more virtuous gathering than this?

It is for this reason that I plead to all parents not to withdraw their children at a young age because of what has been mentioned. A couple of hours of Madrasah a day really can keep Shaytān away!

(Shaykh Yūsuf Motāla Sāhib)

Amazing Advice by the Great Scholar Imām Ibnul Qayyim al-Jawziyyah ﷺ

"A friend will not (literally) share your struggles, a loved one cannot physically take away your pain and a close one will not stay up the night on your behalf. So look after yourself, protect yourself, nurture yourself and do not give life's events more than what they are really worth.

Know for certain that when you break, no one will heal you except you and when you are defeated, no one will give you victory except your determination. Your ability to stand up again and carry on is your responsibility.

Do not look for yourself worth in the eyes of people; look for your worth from within your conscious. If your conscious is at peace, then you will ascend high and if you truly know yourself, then what is said about you will not harm you.

Do not carry the worries of this life because this is for Allāh ﷻ. And do not carry the worries of sustenance because it is from Allāh ﷻ. And do not carry the anxiety of the future because it is in the hands of Allāh ﷻ.

Carry one thing: how to please Allāh ﷻ. Because if you please Him, He Pleases you.

Do not weep for a life that made your heart weep. Just say, "O' Allāh ﷺ, compensate me with good in this life and the Hereafter."

Sadness departs with a Sajdah. Happiness comes with a sincere Du'ā. Allāh ﷺ does not forget the good you do, nor does He forget the good you did to others and the pain you relieved them from, nor will He forget the eye which was about to cry but you made it laugh.

Live your life with this principle: Be good even if you do not receive good, not for others' sakes but because Allāh ﷺ loves those who do good."

Never be Rude and Arrogant to Anyone

An American tourist asked a boat guy in Zanzibar, "Do you know Biology, Psychology, Geography, Geology and Criminology?" The boat guy said, "No, I don't know any of these". The tourist then said "What the hell do you know on the face of this earth? You will die of illiteracy!" The boat guy said nothing.

After a while, the boat developed a fault and started sinking. The boatman then asked the tourist, "Do you know Swimology and Escapology from Crocodilogy?" The tourist said, "No!" The boat guy replied, "Well today you will Drownology and Crocodilogy will eat your biology! I will not Helpology and you will Dieology because of your Badmouthology!"

Colonel Amiruddin Sāhib ﷺ

Colonel Amiruddin Sāhib the Ameer of Canada, born in Edinburgh, Scotland, died on the 18th of September 2012 at the age of 99 in Toronto. He converted over 5500 people to Islām and said he stopped counting to maintain his sincerity. He was a man of complete sincerity and a shining light in these dark times. For over 55 years of his life he travelled more than 72 countries, spending whatever he earned in his life in the path of Allāh ﷻ. His practice was to go in the path of Allāh ﷻ for about 8 months in a year and spend 4 months with his family.

Colonel Amiruddin Sāhib was born to a Scottish lady, Ella Allen later to become Halima Farid-ud-Din, who converted to Islām when she was 16 years old after dreaming of the Ka'bah. She married Nawāb-Farid-ud-Din Khān a descendent of the Prophet ﷺ two years later while he was in Scotland.

Colonel Sāhib was ingrained in the affluent community of Hyderabad under the Nizām Rule. He was a Colonel in the British Army and then the Hyderabad Army. He witnessed the fall, destruction and occupation of Hyderabad by the Indian Army in 1948. Many of these affluent Muslims in Hyderabad started joining the Tableeghi Jamā'at (group of callers to faith) in the 1950's and he was one of them. His life completely transformed and he became a staunch practicing and preaching Muslim. The Nizām of Hyderabad praised him and told him to be steadfast when Colonel Sāhib adopted the visible practices of the Sunnah.

In May 1971, the first Tableeghi Jamā'at from India of 18 people went to Canada and the USA for 4 months. Colonel Sāhib was in this Jamā'at. In the 1970's, Islām was unknown in the USA, Canada and Europe and at the same time, thousands of Muslims were migrating there to earn a livelihood, while being subject to an inferiority complex and slavery mentality due to 100-200 years of colonial rule. Muslims were afraid even to pray Jumu'ah Salāh. The Tableeghi Jamā'at inculcated the spirit of Da'wah (process of inviting to faith) in Muslims. This brought about Muslims practicing Islām, constructing Masājid (Mosques), establishing Musallahs (places of prayer) and Madāris (Islamic schools) and also converting thousands of non-Muslims to Islām in the USA, Canada and Europe.

Colonel Sāhib was initiated into the Naqshbandi Tareeqah (spiritual path) by the Muhaddith of Deccan, Syed Abdullāh Shāh Naqshbandi ؒ and also Maulāna Yūsuf Kandhālvi ؒ. He moved on foot through jungles of Africa, in the heat of Arabia and the bitter cold of Europe to spread Islām.

In one of his lectures he states, "It was the time when there was tension in South Africa between whites and blacks, Jamā'ats were not given permission to enter. Maulāna Yūsuf ؒ said to Colonel Amiruddin Sāhib ؒ, "You are a Colonel and you must find a way to enter into Africa." A plan was made and they walked the jungles of Africa for around 4000 km in the path of Allāh ﷻ which took them 7 months. Only two days had passed when police caught them and put the Jamā'at in jail. People came to know that a Jamā'at has come from India and they began bringing meals to prison. The meals were so many that they were distributed in prison and many of the prisoners accepted Islām by seeing the atmosphere in jail and preachings of the Jamā'at.

Since Colonel Sāhib was a white man, they requested him to leave Africa but he replied, "We want to meet our brothers here." He was then questioned by the leading officer for the reason of coming to Africa. Colonel Sahib took out a pen and paper and then wrote the six points of Tableegh and said, "We have come to learn this."

He was in the Scarborough General Hospital in Toronto, Canada. On Monday, 30 Shawwāl 1433 / 17 September 2012, visitors came and talked to him and recited Qur'ān sitting beside his bed. He was also assisted to pray Zuhr Salāh which was the last prayer of his life. He breathed his last at 5:45 pm on Monday, 30 Shawwāl 1433 / 17 September 2012. Colonel Sāhib was constantly reciting the Kalimah Shahādah and he was insisting visitors to recite it as well and was feeling satisfaction hearing the recitation of it and the Holy Qur'ān.

May Allāh ﷻ protect him from the punishment of the grave and give him Jannatul Firdaus. Āmeen!

Experience of Maulāna Fuād Samaai of Cape Town and His Experience With Colonel Sāhib

We once went in a walking Jamā'at with Colonel Sāhib. Hāji Bhai Padia Sāhib was also in the Jamā'at. We were walking from Lenasia to Potch. We were walking in three groups. On the outskirts of Lenasia the road took a very wide turn. There was a vast open field that ran right alongside that road. Bhai Padia then started walking with his group onto the field as it was a short cut. Colonel Sāhib saw it and shouted, "Bhai Padia Sāhib, go back to the point where you stepped onto the field and walk along the road." Hāji Sāhib was surprised and asked why. Colonel Sāhib said, "Did you get permission from the owners of the field to walk on it? You want to save the walking of a few yards and you can't see its taking you to Jahannam. Go take the permission of the owners first and then take the shortcut." I will never ever forget this incident!

Advice to the Scholars

Mufti Muhammad Rafee Sāhib gave the following three sincere and heart rendering advices to the Ulamā.

1. Ulamā should be engaged in إصلاح باطن (the rectification and purification of the inner self)

2. Ulamā should continue to increase their knowledge and understanding of Islām even after graduation as graduation is merely a sign

that one now has the tools to undertake the never-ending journey to acquire knowledge. There is no limit to knowledge.

3. Ulamā should keep differences within the bounds of academia. Differences should not go beyond that and become personal. There have always been academic differences from the time of the Companions ﷺ upto and including our great scholars of Dārul-Uloom Deoband but they were never personal and they maintained respect and integrity with whomsoever they differed. This is extremely important.

Mufti Muhammad Rafee Sāhib also mentioned that our great scholars of Dārul-Uloom Deoband were so great because they had these three outstanding qualities of perfection:

1. Taqwā - they led a life embedded with Taqwā (piety).

2. Following the Sunnah of the Holy Prophet Muhammad ﷺ.

3. They were completely absolved of any ego. They had completely nullified themselves. There was no 'me'.

Mufti Muhammad Rafee Sāhib also mentioned that to get the proper and complete understanding of the Deen of Islām, a person needs to be proficient and engaged in both types of Fiqh i.e Al-Fiqh Az-Zāhir (Fiqh that is related mainly to the outer actions) and Al-Fiqh Al-Bātin (Fiqh that is related mainly to the inner-actions of the Nafs and soul). Having mere knowledge of Al-Fiqh Az-Zāhir without engaging in the actions related to Al-Fiqh Al-Bātin is a recipe for disaster.

Everybody has a Different Story

A 24-year old man looking out through a train's window shouted, "Dad look, the trees are going behind; they are moving very fast!" His dad simply stared at him with so much joy and smiled! A young couple seated nearby looked at the 24-year old and thought to themselves, he is so grown up but so childish; he must have a mental disorder for his father not to be bothered.

Suddenly, the young man exclaimed again, "Dad look, the clouds are running with us." The couple could not resist and said to the old man, "Why don't you take your son to a good doctor or maybe a psychiatrist?

The old man smiled and said, "I just did. We are just coming from a doctor but not a psychiatrist, we are just coming from the hospital. My son was blind from birth. He just got his sight today for the very first time, his behaviour may seem stupid to you but it is more than a miracle to me." The young couple just sat down there, lost for words with a mixture of tears and shame in their eyes..

Everybody on earth has a story; don't judge people so fast or jump into conclusion about their private affairs; you don't know where they are coming from or what they have to deal with. The truth behind their story might surprise you.

Take it easy with others, even if you have a perfect life. Let us keep working towards the good of all.

Imagine

Imagine sitting with your spouse in Jannah and then deciding what the plans would be for that day…

Should we go outside or sit on our thrones, with waterfalls of milk and honey flowing beneath us and enjoy a cup of Jannah wine, while smelling the sweet scent of Jannah musk?

Should we go to the market place, meet all of our old friends that we used to kick off with in the Dunya and talk about what Dunya was like, how we all made it here and how Allāh ﷻ bestowed His favours upon us?

And then your spouse says, "You know what, how about we go visit the Prophet ﷺ today?" So you and your spouse, go hand in hand, walking towards the house of the Prophet ﷺ.

You pass by the homes of Talha ؓ and Zubair ؓ and you say Salām to them. Then you go and knock on the door of the Prophet ﷺ in Jannah.
Lo and behold, Rasūlullāh ﷺ opens, with a big smile on his face, and says, "welcome", and embraces you.

He invites you to sit inside his home in his noble living room and sits right across from you and asks you if would like a cup of Jannah tea.

You sit in the home of Rasūlullāh ﷺ and he gives you a cup of tea. He sits in front of you and gives you his undivided attention.

Imagine what that discussion would be like… What would you tell him? What would you ask him?

Would you tell him about your favourite moment in the Seerah? Or would you ask him what Tāif was really like? And how he still managed to remember us, as the blood spilled from his noble face?

But in Jannah, there are no more tears and no more fears.... Just the sweetness of success and sacrifices.

Imagine him telling you an inside joke between him and Āishah ؓ . Or the time he caught Anas ؓ playing with kids, instead of running errands.

What if Rasūlullāh ﷺ told you how he remembered you, or how he knew your name and longed for the moment he would meet you?

What if Rasūlullāh ﷺ told you, that he remembers when your Salām reached him, and he answered?

What if, at the end of that conversation, the Prophet ﷺ extended his hand and offered you a sip of water, after which, again you would never feel thirst, not physically nor spiritually....

For the only sight more noble and beautiful than the face of Muhammad ﷺ, is the Face of the Lord of Muhammad ﷺ and the Lord of you.

And for that, all you have to do is look up... and you will see Allāh ﷻ ...

Because in Al Firdaus, you will never be left to imagine again....

Most Hated

The Messenger of Allāh ﷺ said: "The most hated person to Allāh ﷻ is the one who is the most quarrelsome of the opponents." (Bukhāri)

Quarrelling never settles disputes. Distance yourself from quarrels as soon as possible.

Keep this checklist in mind if a quarrel is about to spark off:

1. Let your opponent have the last word. In reality, the one who is quiet is the one who is defended eloquently by Angels.
2. Stop trying to prove that you are right.
3. Accept blame where the fault is yours.
4. State your position just once and then listen.
5. Before the blaming becomes unbearable, politely, either change the topic or physically leave the place of argument.
6. Remember that all cases will be reopened and settled on the Day of Judgement and on that Day none will be able to lie, trick or deceive in any way to support their position.

Ahlul-Bayt (Family of the Prophet ﷺ)

Ahlul-Bayt is best applied to wives even linguistically. The word "Bayt" is from the root بَاتَ يَبِيتُ بَيْتًا meaning to spend the night. So Bayt is a place where one spends the night and hence, Ahlul-bayt are the people one spends the night with. It is really the wife who is a lifetime companion of a person who he spends the night with. Children, sons and daughters, are also included in this concept as they also reside at the Bayt and spent nights there but usually this is only until they move out after marriages. However, it is the wife who remains by a person's side throughout ones life until they separate which is usually at the death of either the husband or the wife.

(Maulānā Ilyās Ghuman)

I'tikāf

I'tikāf means seclusion. There are countless benefits in seclusion, which is why even the Prophets ﷺ used to abandon worldly affairs and sit alone, contemplating upon the favours of Allāh ﷻ and remembering Allāh ﷻ.

Sayyidunā Moosā ﷺ went to Mount Toor and spent 40 days in worship before being gifted with a great scripture like the Tawrah.

Our beloved Prophet ﷺ used to spend time in the cave of Hira before Jibreel ﷺ came with the opening verses of Sūrah 'Alaq. He did not stop going there; he continued to spend time over there even after receiving Prophethood.

Benefits of I'tikāf

Ibn Qudāmah ﷺ writes in Mukhtasar Minhājul-Qāsideen:

There are 6 benefits in spending time in solitude.

1. The first benefit is freedom for worship and proximity to Allāh ﷻ:

One wise man was asked, "What did people benefit from asceticism and from staying alone?" He replied, "Proximity to Allāh ﷻ, Most High." Uwais Qarni ﷺ said, "I would not think that a person would recognise his Lord and then feel Unsiyat (familiarity, intimacy) with someone else."

The aim of staying in seclusion is Dhikr (remembrance of Allāh ﷻ) and Fikr (contemplation). This is why seclusion is more virtuous than mixing with people, as it causes distraction.

2. The second benefit is protecting oneself from sins which could be committed in gatherings.

These sins are of four types;

A) Backbiting: When mixing with people, it is bound to happen. It invites the anger of Allāh ﷻ. Listening to backbiting is also a sin. Sometimes it leads to swearing and abuse as well. By seclusion one can train oneself and cure himself from this evil habit.

B) Riyā (Showing off): When mixing, we tend to do some actions to show people. During seclusion, we get the chance to keep ourselves to ourselves and learn to hide our good deeds from people. Riyā is a huge sickness and is very hard to cure.

C) When mixing, we are required to enjoin good and forbid evil. Yet many times we see evil but we shy away from saying anything, which is a form of disobedience and thus a sin. By staying in seclusion one can protect himself from this sin.

D) In free mixing we tend to pick up bad habits from people. The environment is pretty much out of control. Sin is not only easy, it is made to look good and people are encouraged to sin as much as possible. This is a devilish trait. To get away from Shaytān, we need to sit alone and contemplate over the purpose of life and learn how to behave properly.

3. The third benefit of seclusion is saving oneself from Fitnahs (trials) and fights. During times of Fitnah, we are told to control our tongues, stay in our homes and cry over our sins. This is what will benefit our hearts and keep us safe.

4. The fourth benefit is saving oneself from the evils of the community. People are very cunning. They trick you, accuse you, slander you, back bite you and make fun of you behind your back. Staying away from people protects one from these evils. Sayyidunā Umar ؓ says, "In seclusion there is safety from evil company."

5. The fifth benefit is that when one stays away from people, they lose hope from him and he loses hope from them. People do not pay much attention to those who keep themselves to themselves. They do not invite such people to Waleemahs, Da'wats, functions, etc. When one keeps mixing with people, he develops love for the material world, gets greedy, wants more money, flashy cars, designer clothes and a luxurious life etc. By sitting in seclusion one can lose all these vain hopes and get some contentment of the heart.

One Hadeeth says, "Look at those who are below you, not at those who are above you. This will teach you not to belittle the blessings of Allāh ﷻ upon you."

6. The sixth benefit is saving oneself from socialising with foolish people within the society. There are plenty of them out there. Many are lazy couch potatoes. They do not do anything good and do not let anyone else do it. When one is tested by such people, he will definitely get angry at some stage, speak ill of them and mention their insults to others. This leads to Deeni destruction. In seclusion there is safety from this. (Minhāj pg89/90)

Imām Bukhāri ﷺ says:

$$\text{لِقَاءُ النَّاسِ لَيْسَ يُفِيْدُ شَيْئاً}$$
$$\text{سِوَي الْهُذْيَانِ مِنْ قِيْلَ وَقَالَ}$$
$$\text{فَأَقْلِلْ لِقَاءَ النَّاسِ اِلَّا}$$
$$\text{لِأَخْذِ عِلْمٍ أَوْ إِصْلَاحِ حَالٍ}$$

There is no benefit in meeting with people
besides gossip of 'he said, it is being said'
Therefore, reduce your connection with people except
for seeking knowledge or spiritual remedy.

May Allāh ﷻ give us the Tawfeeq (ability) to detach ourselves from the Dunyā and attach ourselves with Allāh ﷻ Most High. Āmeen.

Values

When the ancient Chinese decided to live in peace, they made the great wall of China. They thought no one can climb it due to its height.

During the first 100 year of its existence, the Chinese were invaded thrice.

And every time, the hordes of enemy infantry had no need of penetrating or climbing over the wall because each time, they bribed the guards and came through the doors.

The Chinese built the wall but forgot the character-building of the wall-guards. Thus, the building of human character comes before the building of anything else..... That's what our students need today.

Like one of the Orientalists said:

If you want to destroy the civilization of a nation, there are 3 ways:

1. Destroy their family structure.
2. Destroy their education system.
3. Lower their role models and references.

1.In order to destroy the family, undermine the role of motherhood; make her feel ashamed of being a housewife.

2. To destroy the education system, you should give no importance to the teacher and lower his place in society so that the students despise him.

3. To lower the role models, you should undermine their scholars and doubt them until no one listens to them or trusts them.

For when a conscious mother disappears, a dedicated teacher disappears and there is a downfall of role models, who will teach the youngsters VALUES?

Give it a thought! Is our home also invaded?

Solidarity With Refugees

A famine struck Madeenah Munawwarah during the Caliphate of Umar ﷺ. Because of serious famine conditions, the people were involved in great distress. Sayyidunā Umar ﷺ rose to the occasion. He wrote to the provincial governors asking them to send food grains to Arabia. Camel loads of food grains and other necessities of life came from other parts of the Muslim lands, Syria, Iraq and Egypt. Food grains were received from Egypt by sea also.

In view of the resources at his disposal, Sayyidunā Umar ﷺ could afford to have any food, but he vowed that as long as the famine lasted, he would eat only what was available to a person of ordinary means. He refused to eat meat, ghee or butter during the period of famine. He would eat only the coarsest of food. As a consequence of eating nutrition-less food, his colour and appearance changed. His stomach would rumble, but he said: "O stomach! you may rumble as much as you like, but as long as the famine persists, I cannot allow you anything dainty."

One day, some ghee came to the market and his servant purchased the ghee for him. He refused it saying, "How can I be concerned for the people if I do not suffer what they suffer?"

The people on the other hand were so concerned for Sayyidunā Umar ؓ that they would say, "O' Allāh ﷻ! Weaken the severity of famine. We fear Sayyidunā Umar ؓ would die worrying about the difficulties of the Muslims." [Tāreekh at Tabari 2/508]

Sayyidunā Umar ؓ possessed a heart that was towering, lofty and full of mercy. Today, Muslim leaders possess numerous lofty towers but have hearts devoid of any compassion and mercy.

The Fly and Antibiotics

What is in a wing of a fly that led our Noble Prophet Muhammad ﷺ to say, "If a fly falls in the vessel of any of you, let him dip all of it (into the vessel) and then throw it away, for in one of its wings there is a disease and in the other there is healing (antidote for it)." (Bukhārī)

Well, let us look at this short article:

The New Buzz on Antibiotics
Danny Kingsley - ABC Science Online

The surface of flies is the last place you would expect to find antibiotics, yet that is exactly where a team of Australian researchers is concentrating their efforts. Working on the theory that flies must have remarkable antimicrobial defences to survive rotting dung, meat and fruit, the team at the Department of Biological Sciences, Macquarie University, set out to identify those antibacterial properties manifesting at different stages of a fly's development.

"Our research is a small part of a global research effort for new antibiotics, but we are looking where we believe no-one has looked before," said Ms Joanne Clarke, who presented the group's findings at the Australian Society for Microbiology Conference in Melbourne this week. The project is part of her PhD thesis.

The scientists tested four different species of fly: a house fly, a sheep blowfly, a vinegar fruit fly and a Queensland fruit fly which lays its eggs in fresh fruit. These larvae do not need as much antibacterial compound because they do not come into contact with as much bacteria.

Flies go through the life stages of larvae and pupae before becoming adults. In the pupae stage, the fly is encased in a protective casing and does not feed. "We predicted they would not produce many antibiotics," said Ms Clarke. They did not. However the larvae all showed antibacterial properties (except that of the Queensland fruit fly control). As did all the adult fly species, including the Queensland fruit fly (which at this point requires antibacterial protection because it has contact with other flies and is mobile). Such properties were present on the fly surface in all four species, although antibacterial properties occur in the gut as well. "You find activity in both places," said Ms Clarke.

"The reason we concentrated on the surface is because it is a simpler extraction." The antibiotic material is extracted by drowning the flies in ethanol, then running the mixture through a filter to obtain the crude extract.

When this was placed in a solution with various bacteria including E.coli, Golden Staph, Candida (a yeast) and a common hospital pathogen, antibiotic action was observed every time.

"We are now trying to identify the specific antibacterial compounds," said Ms Clarke. Ultimately, these will be chemically synthesised. Because the compounds are not from bacteria, any genes conferring resistance to them may not be as easily transferred into pathogens. It is hoped this new form of antibiotics will have a longer effective therapeutic life.

فَتَبَارَكَ اللهُ أَحْسَنُ الْخَالِقِيْنَ

So Glory be to Allāh, the Best of Creators.

Message for Muslims in the West

Shaykh Sayyid Abul Hasan Ali Nadwi's ﷺ summary of a speech delivered in Urdu at Markaz, Dewsbury in 1982.

Your warm reception and friendliness is a source of great happiness for me. If I do not respect your wishes and express my inner feelings, I would be most ungrateful. If I desire, I could shower you with praises, for Almighty Allāh ﷺ has bestowed me with an abundance of vocabulary, but I would not be fulfilling the right of friendship.

As you are aware, the Prophet ﷺ had a burning desire to invite humanity to accept Islām. Despite 13 years of untiring effort in Makkah Mukarramah and 7 years in Madeenah Munawwarah, there was no large scale conversion of non-Muslims into Islām. However, between 7 AH and 10 AH, after Fath-Makkah (conquest of Makkah) until the

Prophet's ﷺ demise, there was such an influx of people entering into Islām as was not witnessed in the preceding 20 years.

Imām Zuhri ؓ, an eminent Muhaddith and Tābi'ee, expresses surprise on this sea of change, with so many people embracing Islām in a matter of just 3 years. He, along with other distinguished Muhaddithoon, have commented that this large scale conversion was due to non-Muslims having an opportunity, for the first time, to observe and intermingle with Muslims, witnessing their honesty, fair dealing, compassion, and their sole reliance on Allāh ﷻ. This left such a deep and profound impression on non-Muslims that thousands entered into the fold of Islām within a relatively short period of time.

This incident also contains abundant lessons on how Muslims should live in this country. Their conduct should be so sublime and captivating that whosoever sees us, accepts Islām. Whosoever sits with us should be inclined towards Islām. There should be no need to convince anyone to accept the Truth.

Therefore, in this country, if you wish to live peacefully and have an opportunity to present Islām to the host community, you will need to inculcate and manifest brilliant qualities, not just inside the Masājid but also outside in the streets, in the markets, in your daily activities and at home. A life of Taqwā will immediately attract non-Muslims towards Islām.

As an ordinary student of Islām, it is my religious responsibility to warn you. If you do not lead an upright life, if you continue to live a narrow-minded lifestyle, and if you fail to manifest the beauty of Islām to non-Muslims, then you will face real dangers. In such a case, there is no reason for you to feel content and secure in this country.

If ever the fire of race, religion or nationalism rages here, then you will not be saved. In Spain, there were Masājid a hundred times more beautiful than yours, so do not feel content and self-satisfied. As an ordinary student of religion, I would wish to express my joy and happiness at this wonderful new Masjid, but how shall I congratulate you on your achievement, when the words of congratulation are self-evident on the walls. How better can I compliment you?

Others may not speak to you as plainly, but remember the glorious Masjid-e-Cordova still stands in Spain. Iqbal so eloquently reminisces the great legacy of Islamic Spain in his famous poem 'Masjid-e-Qurtuba'. In Islamic Spain there were such brilliant Masājid, celebrated Madāris and famous scholars, for instance Shaikh-e-Akbar, Ibn Hazm, Qurtubi, Shātbi - and how many others shall I mention? However, when the flames of religious sectarianism raged, then the Masājid and Madāris became deserted. Once, Islamic Spain boasted such magnificent structures, distinguished educational centres, and a refined culture and society. Regrettably, the Muslims, despite such a high standard of living, did not draw the native non-Muslims of that country to see the truth of Islām and warn them of the dangers of disbelief, with the result that religions subsequently consumed Muslims like a morsel. The Arabs, with their glowing history, architectural splendour and vast ocean of knowledge, were displaced from the country and today, the ears eagerly wait to hear the Adhān and the empty Masājid thirst for your Salāh.

You must earn your place in this country. You should leave an imprint on the host community of your usefulness. You must demonstrate that your existence here is more beneficial than that of the native people. You must impart on them the lessons of humanity. You should demonstrate how noble and principled you are, and that there cannot be found more upright humans elsewhere besides you. You need to establish your worth and that you are a blessing and mercy for this country. However, if you decide to live in an enclosed environment, content with your prayers and fasting, apathetic to the people and society you live in and never introducing them to the high Islamic values and your own personal qualities, then beware, lest any religion or sectarianism flares up. In such a situation you will not find safety.

I pray to Almighty Allāh ﷻ that my prediction is totally untrue and baseless. Remember, you are guests here. Your Tableegh, Masājid, Madāris, Ibādah and religious sacrifices are all worthy of commendation. May Almighty Allāh ﷻ grant you Barakah, but do not forget to earn your place in this country. Gain mastery of the national language and become proficient so that you can use it effectively to propagate Islām. Prepare writers and orators and although you will distance yourself from their religion, do not distance yourself from them. Earn credibility through your daily activities, so much so that if you are entrusted with difficult responsibilities, as was Prophet Yūsuf ﷺ, you do not avoid but embrace all challenges wholeheartedly.

You will have to present a new pattern of life to this country. You will not earn recognition by exerting yourselves in the workplace. If you overwork, you will be looked upon disparagingly and be likened to horses and bulls and labelled as money-making machines. However, if you can show to the natives here that you are worshippers of Allāh ﷻ and not wealth, that you do not bow before power but only before virtue, that you are humans and think like humans, that you are concerned not only about yourselves but also about others, that you are compassionate not just to your own children but also to theirs and to them, and that you are earnestly concerned about the path of destruction they have chosen for themselves then you will earn their respect. They will begin to respect Islām and become desirous of studying it. They will ask you for literature concerning Islamic beliefs and practices and an opportunity will arise here for you to propagate Islām.

However, if you remain preoccupied in eating and working and engaged in prayers, indifferent to what is happening in the country, insulated within Muslims and totally apathetic to what is happening outside and which direction the country is heading, in such a situation, if there is any trouble, you will not be able to save yourselves.

I have been meaning to convey and emphasise this message to you, because I do not know whether I will be able to visit you in the future. You gathered here with love and affection and therefore it was easy for me. As a student of religion, it would have been convenient for me to suggest virtues of reciting various Dhikr or prescribe certain Wazeefahs, but you might not have had an opportunity of listening to the message I have just conveyed from anyone else.

Please strengthen your position in this country and earn your recognition. Do not be like a straw or crop that is uprooted by the slightest breeze. You should be so firm that not even a hurricane is able to shift you. Display such noble character that you enslave the natives, then see how these people will stand to defend you. If there is the slightest opposition against you, they will be the first ones to argue on your behalf and vouch what a blessing you are for them.

May Almighty Allāh ﷻ grant us the ability to understand what is right; may He bless and protect you. Āmeen.

I Hear the Salām of a Zā'ir (Visitor) at My Grave

Sayyidunā Abū Hurairah ؓ reports that Rasūlullāh ﷺ said: "When a person stands at my grave reciting Durood (blessings) on me, I hear it; and whoever calls for blessings on me in any other place, his need in this world and the Hereafter is fulfilled and on the Day of Qiyāmah, I shall be his witness and intercessor. [Baihaqi]

According to another Hadeeth, Allāh ﷻ has appointed a special angel whose duty is to take the recited 'Durood' to Rasūlullāh ﷺ, so no matter where the Durood is being recited, it reaches Rasūlullāh ﷺ in Madeenah.

How great virtue it is if one should stand reciting the Durood at the grave where Rasūlullāh ﷺ can personally hear it, and how fortunate are those who live in Madeenah Munawwarah, whose greetings Rasūlullāh ﷺ hears at all times without any go-between!

Sulaimān Ibn Suhaim ؓ says: "I once saw Rasūlullāh ﷺ in my dream and enquired of him: 'O Messenger of Allāh ﷺ, Are you aware when people come before your grave and recite Durood on you?' Rasūlullāh ﷺ replied: 'Yes, I am quite aware of it and I reply to their greetings.'"

Khālid Ibn Ma'dān ؓ says, "I performed Hajj and then visited Madeenah. When I approached the Rawdhah (grave) and offered my Salām, I heard, 'Wa Alaikas-Salām', from the Rawdhah."

When Shaykh Sayyid Husain Ahmad Madani ؓ (a descendant of the Holy Prophet ﷺ) came and said, "Assalāmu-Alaika Yā Jaddi, Yā Rasūlallāh ﷺ," (greetings upon you O' my Grandfather, O' Messenger of Allāh ﷺ) he heard, "Wa Alaikas Salām Yā Waladi (greetings upon you O' my son)."

The story of Sayyid Ahmad Rifāi ﷺ is well documented. It is narrated by Imām Suyooti ﷺ in 'Al-Hāwi' that when Sayyid Ahmad Rifāi ﷺ approached the Rawdhah and recited two couplets, two hands appeared. He kissed them and then they disappeared.

The couplets were:

في حالة البعد روحي كنت ارسلها
تقبل الارض مني وهي نائبتي
هذا اوان للأشباح قد حضرت
فامدد يديك لكي تحظي بها شفتي

"While I was at a distance, I would send my soul,
Which would kiss this land, the soul was my deputy,

Now that my body limbs are here,
Could you please stretch your hands so that my lips can become fortunate."

Shaykh Zakariyya ﷺ has mentioned many such incidents in his beautiful book 'Virtues of Hajj'; denying them is denying history altogether.

A friend of mine who lives in London related his experience. He told me not to disclose his name so I will just call him Abdullāh. He is a very good Hāfiz of the Holy Qur'ān and a beautiful reciter.

He says I would recite a lot of Durood. While travelling on the tube, people would be busy with their things. I would take out 40 Salawāt and read them through the journey.

When I came for Umrah and arrived at Madeenah, I came to Riyādhul-Jannah. I prayed a few Rak'ats Nafl. Then I closed my eyes and I was so much in awe that I just began to say, "Assalāmu-Alaika Yā Rasūlallāh." I heard with my own ears, "Wa Alaikas-Salām Yā Abdallāh" I opened my eyes and looked around. There was no one there who knew my name.

May Allāh ﷻ give us the ability to recognise the status of Rasūlullāh ﷺ and to revere and respect him as he deserves.

May Allāh ﷻ deliver the choicest blessings and greetings to His beloved Prophet ﷺ, our Leader, our Master, our Guide, Muhammad ﷺ. Āmeen.

Sayyidunā Uthmān ☙

All Sahābah ☙ are noble, special and honourable, and why should they not be so, after all they are the Companions and direct students of the best of the creation, the Imām and seal of the Prophets and the beloved Prophet of Allāh ﷺ, Muhammad ﷺ.

Uthmān Ibn Affān ☙ is not just a Sahābi; he was a nephew of the Prophet ﷺ (as his maternal grandmother, Umme Hakeem Bint Abdul Muttalib was the twin sister of the Prophet's ﷺ father, Abdullāh). He was 'Zun-Noorain', (the one with two lights), blessed and honoured to have been married to two daughters of the Prophet ﷺ. Just as those with daughters want to wed them to the best young man they can find, do we not think that Rasūlullāh ﷺ wanted to wed two of his daughters to the best man he could find for this honour?

He was also a Khalifah Rāshid (Guided Caliph). In the Qur'ān, in Surah Noor, verse 55, Allāh ﷻ has stated, **"And Allāh has promised those who believe from amongst you and do good deeds that he will definitely grant them Khilāfah of the earth."**

This verse endorses the honour of Sayyidunā Uthmān ☙ in that among the other Khulafā, he received Khilāfah as a result of a direct and personal promise of Allāh ﷻ. This verse also endorses and confirms the Imān and good deeds of all the Khulafā, including Sayyidunā Uthmān ☙.

As well as having given Sayyidunā Uthmān ؓ glad tidings and assurance of Paradise on many different occasions, the Prophet ﷺ also informed him of his eventual death as a Shaheed (martyr).

$$\text{اِنَّ رَسُوْلَ اللهِ صَلَّى اللهُ عَلَيْهِ وَسَلَّمَ صَعِدَ اُحُدًا وَاَبُوْ بَكْرٍ وَعُمَرُ وَعُثْمَانُ فَرَجَفَ بِهِمْ فَقَالَ رَسُوْلُ اللهِ صَلَّى اللهُ عَلَيْهِ وَسَلَّمَ : اُثْبُتْ اُحُدُ فَاِنَّمَا عَلَيْكَ نَبِيٌّ وَصِدِّيْقٌ وَشَهِيْدَانِ}$$

Once the Prophet ﷺ climbed Mount Uhud along with Abū Bakr, Umar and Uthmān, and it (Mount Uhud) began shaking. So the Prophet ﷺ said, "Uhud! Be calm! For upon you is a Nabi, a Siddeeq and two Shaheeds." (Tirmizi)

Shahādah (martyrdom) is such an honour that Allāh ﷻ says,

$$\text{وَلَا تَقُوْلُوْا لِمَنْ يُّقْتَلُ فِيْ سَبِيْلِ اللهِ اَمْوَاتٌ بَلْ اَحْيَاءٌ وَّلٰكِنْ لَّا تَشْعُرُوْنَ}$$

"And do not speak about those killed in the path of Allāh as dead; rather they are alive but you do not understand."(2:154)

In another verse Allāh ﷻ says,

$$\text{وَلَا تَحْسَبَنَّ الَّذِيْنَ قُتِلُوْا فِيْ سَبِيْلِ اللهِ اَمْوَاتًا بَلْ اَحْيَاءٌ عِنْدَ رَبِّهِمْ يُرْزَقُوْنَ}$$

"And do not even consider those killed in the path of Allāh as dead, rather they are alive in the presence of their Lord and are given sustenance." (3:169)

So Sayyidunā Uthmān ﷺ, was so fortunate that he enjoyed such nobility; as they say نور على نور (goodness upon goodness).

A Sahābi ﷺ, double son in-law of the Prophet ﷺ, a Muhājir (migrant), a Khaleefah-Rāshid and a Shaheed. How many can boast a C.V like Uthmān ﷺ?

A Perfect Poem Written in the Saddest Way.

"I destroy homes, tear families apart,
Take your children, and that's just the start.

I'm more costly than diamonds, more costly than gold,
The sorrow I bring is a sight to behold.

And if you need me, remember I'm easily found,
I live in schools and in towns, I am always around.

I live with the rich, I live with the poor,
I live down the street, and maybe next door.

My power is awesome, try me you'll see,
But if you do, you may never break free.

Just try me once and I might let you go,
but try me twice, and I'll own your soul.

When I possess you, you'll steal and you'll lie,
You'll do what you have to, just to get high.

The crimes you'll commit, for my narcotic charms,
Will be worth the pleasure, you'll feel in your arms.

You'll lie to your mother, you'll steal from your dad,
When you see their tears, you won't feel sad.

But you'll forget your morals and how you were raised,
I'll be your conscience, I'll teach you my ways.

I take kids from parents, and parents from kids,
I turn people from God, and separate from friends.

I'll take everything from you, your looks and your pride,
I'll always be with you, right by your side.

You'll give up everything - your family, your home,
Your friends, your money, and then you'll be all alone.

Gems and Jewels   A Perfect Poem

I'll take and I'll take, till you have nothing more to give,
When I'm finished with you, you'll be lucky to live.

If you try me, be warned, this is no game,
If given the chance, I'll drive you insane.

I'll ravish your body, I'll control your mind,
I'll own you completely; your soul will be mine.

The nightmares I'll give you while lying in bed,
The voices you'll hear from inside your head.

The sweats, the shakes, the visions you'll see,
I want you to know, these are all gifts from me.

But then it's too late, and you'll know in your heart,
That you are mine, and we shall not part.

You'll regret that you tried me, they always do,
But you came to me, not I to you.

You knew this would happen, many times you were told,
But you challenged my power, and chose to be bold.

You could have said no, and just walked away,
If you could live that day over now, what would you say?

I'll be your master, you will be my slave,
I'll even go with you, when you go to your grave.

Now that you have met me, what will you do?
Will you try me or not? Its all up to you.

I can bring you more misery than words can tell,
Come take my hand, let me lead you to hell."

Sign: DRUGS

The Best Season for the Believer

"Winter is the best season for the believer because Allāh ﷻ strengthens his practice by making worship easy for him. The believer can easily fast during the day without suffering from hunger and thirst. The days are short and cold and he does not feel the hardship of fasting.

As for praying at night, due to winter's long nights, one can have his share of sleep and then wake up to pray. He can recite the Qur'ān that he usually does in the day, while having enough time to sleep.

So, it becomes possible to fulfil the interest of both his religion and the comfort of his body.

Sayyidunā Abdullāh Ibn Mas'ood ﷺ said: "Welcome to winter! Blessings descend in it. Its nights are long to pray, and its days are short to fast."

When it was winter, Ubaid Ibn Umair ﷺ would say: "O people of the Qur'ān! Your nights are now long for you to recite. So, recite! Your days are now short for you to fast. So, fast! Night prayer in the winter equals fasting during the day in the summer."

This is why Sayyidunā Mu'ādh ﷺ wept on his deathbed. He said: "I weep because I will miss the thirst I felt when I fasted and I will miss praying at night during the winter and sitting knee to knee with the scholars during the gatherings of knowledge."

(Ibn Rajab Hanbali ﷺ)

Fasting on the 10th of Muharram

Some say it is Makrooh (disliked) to fast only on the 10th of Muharram, and that one should only fast on the 10th if one will be fasting on the 9th or the 11th too. Although it is best to fast either on all three days i.e. 9th, 10th and 11th, or on two of the three days i.e. 9th and 10th, or 10th and 11th, it is not correct to label fasting just on the 10th as Makrooh and to tell people who fast on the 10th only not to fast at all.

This is because Rasūlullāh ﷺ fasted on just the 10th throughout his lifetime and had expressed his desire to fast on the 9th also if he were to live until the next year. However, this did not transpire. Thus, the statement of the Fuqahā that it is Makrooh to fast on the 10th of Muharram on its own will be interpreted as fasting only on the 10th to be less in virtue compared to fasting on other days alongside the 10th.

Spending on the Day of Āshoorā

Excerpts from 'The Beauty of Prophet Muhammad ﷺ in Light of Lessons in Saheeh Bukhāri', authored by Shaykhul-Hadeeth Shaykh Yūsuf Motāla Sāhib.

- A Narration Regarding Āshoorā

I was remembering the day of Āshoorā today. I spent so many Āshoorās in Shaykh Zakariyyā's company during my twenty year period with him. There are enough stories [pertaining to the Shaykh] regarding this day that a small book could be written. There are very few amongst us who will not be familiar with the following Hadeeth on Āshoorā.

Regarding 10th Muharram, Rasūlullāh ﷺ states:

من وسع على عياله في يوم عاشوراء.

وسَّع الله عليه السنة كلّها.

'He who is generous to his family on the day of Āshoorā, Allāh ﷻ will increase his provisions (grant prosperity) throughout the year.' [Baihaqī]

The likes of Sufyān Ibn Uyaynah ؓ, regarding the above Hadeeth states, 'I have been doing this for fifty to sixty years and have always seen its benefit.'

- The Gift of Āshūrā: A Practice of Shaykh Zakariyyā ؒ

The year in which we studied the Saheeh Bukhārī under Shaykh Zakariyyā ؒ, we saw that it was his practice to distribute money to his household (children, daughters, grandsons, grand-daughters and everybody else) just as we distribute gifts on Eid. The gift of Āshoorā was something they received every year. Feasting with an abundance of food and drink was witnessed.

The Shaykh would also ask for a [rupee] coin to be brought for every Dawrah-Hadeeth (final year) student. He once gave me the bag full of coins to distribute among my peers and, once I had done so, he said, "Okay, you take one as well." After I took a coin, he said, "Take one more."

Incidents During Muharram

2AH - Nikāh of Sayyidunā Ali ؓ with Sayyidah Fātimah ؓ
3AH - Nikāh of Sayyidah Umme Kulthūm ؓ with Sayyidunā Uthmān ؓ
7AH - Sending out invitation letters to various kings
7AH - Battle of Khaybar
9AH - Establishment of Nizāme Zakāt (system of Zakāt) by sending out Zakāt collectors
18AH - Plague of Amwās (Syria, in which hundreds of Sahābah ؓ died)
21AH - Egypt conquered by Sayyidunā Amr Ibn Ās ؓ
24AH - 1st Muharram - Shahādah of Sayyidunā Umar ؓ
24AH - 4th Muharram - Khilāfat of Sayyidunā Uthmān ؓ
36AH - Khilāfat of Sayyidunā Ali ؓ
45AH - The Conquest of Africa
51AH - Death of Abū Ayyūb Ansāri ؓ
55AH - Death of Sa'd Ibn Abi Waqqās ؓ
61AH - 10th Muharram - Shahādah of Sayyidunā Husain Ibn Ali ؓ
74AH - Death of Abdullāh Ibn Umar ؓ
133AH - Banū Umayyah's rule comes to an end
137AH - Mansoor Al-Abbāsi's Khilāfat
169AH - Death of Khaleefah Mahdi Abbāsi
321AH - Death of Imām Abū Ja'far Tahāwi ؒ
360AH - Fātimiyyah taking control over Damascus
656AH - Halāku Khan destroying the city of Baghdad
664AH - 5th Muharram - Death of Fareeduddeen Ganjshakar ؒ

1195AH - Shahādat of Mirza Mazhar Jānejānan ﷺ
1283AH - 15th Muharram-Foundation of Dārul-Uloom Deoband (May 1866)
1351AH - Death of Shaykh Anwar Shah Kashmeeri ﷺ (May 1922)

Source: 'Islāmi Maheenow ke Ahkām' by Maulāna Roohullāh

True Love

Somebody asked Sayyidunā Ali ﷺ, "How much was the Sahābahs' ﷺ love for the Holy Prophet ﷺ?" He replied, "By Allāh ﷻ! To us, the Holy Prophet ﷺ was dearer than our riches, our children and our mothers and was more cherished than a drink of cold water at the time of severe thirst."

There was no exaggeration in Sayyidunā Ali's ﷺ statement. As a matter of fact, the Sahābah ﷺ reached this state because of the perfection of their Imān.

The Ulamā have listed many signs which demonstrate love for the Holy Prophet ﷺ. Qādhi Iyādh ﷺ states that if a person loves a thing, then he gives it preference over all things, otherwise, that claim is mere lip-service. Love for the Holy Prophet ﷺ is demonstrated by a few simple and important factors which are to follow in his footsteps, choose his path and obey his statements and actions. One should bring into action the injunctions of the Holy Prophet ﷺ. He should abstain from that which the Holy Prophet ﷺ prohibited. He should follow the Sunnah in all conditions – happiness, grief, affluence and poverty.

I would like to mention an incident from the life of the Sahābah ؓ which will clearly demonstrate their true and intense love for the Holy Prophet ﷺ. When the treaty of Hudaibiyah was taking place, the Quraish of Makkah sent Urwah Ibn Mas'ood Thaqafi to speak to the Holy Prophet ﷺ. Urwa was a very intelligent and observant person. As soon as he came to the Muslim camp, he looked at everything very carefully and even while talking to the Holy Prophet ﷺ, he took notice of how the Sahābah ؓ behaved.

When he went back to the Quraish in Makkah, he had the following to say about how the Sahābah ؓ would even give their lives for the Holy Prophet ﷺ. He said, "O' my people! I have been sent to the kings of Rome, Persia and Abyssinia. However, I swear by Allāh ﷻ that I have never seen the companions of anyone show as much respect to their king as I have seen the Companions of Muhammad ﷺ show to him. I swear by Allāh ﷻ that even when he spits, one of them puts out his hand to get it. When he makes Wudhu, they compete with each other to get the water falling off his body and when he gives a command, they run to carry it out. When he speaks, they all become silent and they always look at him with great love and affection."

It is difficult to use better words than these to explain the respect and love the Sahābah ؓ showed to the Holy Prophet ﷺ. When a person is praised by his enemy, the words carry much more weight. Blessed were those people who managed to soften the hard hearts of their enemies by their excellent behaviour and manner.

May Allāh ﷻ inculcate the true love of the Holy Prophet ﷺ in our daily lives so that we can become successful like the Sahābah ؓ. May Allāh ﷻ give us the Tawfeeq (strength) to carry out the Sunnats and become the true friends of Allāh ﷻ. Āmeen!

And our last call is that all praise is for Allāh ﷻ, the Lord of the Worlds.

The Last Day the Prophet ﷺ Smiled!

There are many narrations that have mentioned that the Holy Prophet ﷺ smiled generously to the people during his Prophethood and even before he became a Prophet.

Have you ever thought of that day when the Ummah last saw the Holy Prophet ﷺ smile?

Here's a story that highlights the love of the Holy Prophet ﷺ for the Sahābah ؓ. It is just so beautiful, Subhān-Allāh.

During the last days of the final illness of the Holy Prophet ﷺ, he became so sick that when it was time for prayer, he could not lead the prayer. So he ordered Sayyidunā Abū Bakr ؓ to lead the prayers.

Sayyidunā Abū Bakr ؓ continued to lead the people in prayer until Monday, when the Holy Prophet ﷺ removed the screen of his apartment, just as the Muslims were busy lining up for prayer. While they were praying, he lay there watching them and appreciating how far they had come in recent years.

Just as a carpenter gives his work a final look of appraisal, the Prophet ﷺ was looking at the finished products of his many years of toil and sacrifice.

He was greatly pleased because he was looking at people who were devotedly performing congregational prayer, without his supervision. The Holy Prophet's ﷺ heart was content, for this was something no other Prophet ﷺ had achieved before him.

The Holy Prophet ﷺ was reassured that after his death, his Sahābah ؓ would continue where he left off. Such thoughts filled the Holy Prophet ﷺ with joy, made his face radiant with happiness, and gave him the strength to stand up.

Meanwhile, the Sahābah ؓ said, "The Prophet ﷺ has removed the screen of Sayyidah Ā'ishah's ؓ apartment and is looking at us while he is standing up." Furthermore, they saw that the Holy Prophet ﷺ was smiling.

Out of love for the Holy Prophet ﷺ, some people mistook this as a sign of his recovery. They thought that he was coming out to lead them in prayer but he signalled to them that they should complete their prayer. He then entered the apartment and lowered the screen.

Subhān-Allāh. Imagine that moment; that precious moment where you see the face of the Holy Prophet ﷺ smiling because he sees you doing your obligations.
How beautiful was that moment.

One can just imagine how his face would have lit and smiled generously.

Now, I ask you to have a moment with yourself and ponder about the things that you have been doing; all the missed Salāhs, the way you have been disrespecting your parents all the time. Do you think you will earn such status when you finally return back to Allāh ﷻ, with all these bad deeds you have been doing?

My brothers and sisters in Islām, it is up to us how we earn Paradise. Yes, we need the guidance, protection, blessings and forgiveness of Allāh ﷻ, but before any of that, we have to have the will to become better and become closer to Him.
Ponder hard.

There's still time to change to be better. If you are faltering on your Salāh, then get up and prepare for the next Salāh right now;

make Wudhu and feed your soul with the Holy Qur'ān.

If you have talked bad about someone, then make use of your phone, call that person and ask for forgiveness. If you have answered back to your parents, then right now, get up and ask for their forgiveness; do not ever let a moment pass that you do not settle things with them.

May Allāh ﷻ accept our good deeds and forgive us and grant us the ranks of the righteous, in companionship with His Messenger ﷺ and finally, witness that smile that the Sahābah ؓ saw. Āmeen!

Sūfism

I start with the name of Allāh ﷻ and by sending my salutations on the greatest Prophet, Muhammad ﷺ, the perfect, the noble. The sad state of affairs of the Muslims of this day and age is that generally, when unlearned people hear the words 'Tasawwuf, Sūfism or Sūfi,' then Bid'ah and misguided sects comes to mind. I am therefore, writing this short article to remove all incorrect beliefs and wrong opinions regarding such a sacred science, which may have come about because of certain fraudulent imposters, who have twisted its beautiful essence and have taken advantage of it to fulfil their own evil desires. I also intend on sharing with you, respectable readers, the proofs from the blessed Qur'ān and noble Ahādeeth.

Everybody will agree that Tafseer, Hadeeth and Fiqh are great branches of Islām. However, we generally seem to neglect one major branch; the branch of spirituality (Tasawwuf, also known as Tazkiyah). The aim of Tasawwuf is reformation of the inner-self (Nafs). It is achieved by perfecting ones character, increasing ones love for Allāh ﷻ (which is assisted by the means of Adhkār) and as an end-result, becoming a close friend of Allāh ﷻ (Wali-e-Kāmil). This was also the aim of the Noble Prophet Muhammad ﷺ who was sent to the honourable Sahābah ؓ when their inner spiritual states were at the peak of degeneration. We are all familiar of the change the Sahābah ؓ underwent from the days of ignorance to the advent of Islām. They transformed from the worst of people to the noblest after the Prophets. They endured a rigorous spiritual rectification (Islāh) process at the hands of the greatest Shaykh, the Noble Prophet Muhammad ﷺ himself.

But why was there a need to rectify them? Why didn't the Noble Prophet Muhammad ﷺ simply teach them the Qur'ān and Hadeeth and go? The answer is simple and is found in the Noble Qur'ān. Allāh ﷻ says,

لَقَدْ مَنَّ اللّٰهُ عَلَى الْمُؤْمِنِيْنَ إِذْ بَعَثَ فِيْهِمْ رَسُوْلًا مِّنْ أَنْفُسِهِمْ يَتْلُوْ عَلَيْهِمْ آيَاتِهٖ وَيُزَكِّيْهِمْ وَيُعَلِّمُهُمُ الْكِتَابَ وَالْحِكْمَةَ وَإِنْ كَانُوْا مِنْ قَبْلُ لَفِيْ ضَلَالٍ مُّبِيْنٍ

"Certainly, did Allāh confer (great) favour upon the believers when He sent among them a Messenger from themselves, reciting to them His verses, teaching them the Book and wisdom and purifying them, although they had been before in manifest error." (3:164)

This verse clearly states that the Noble Prophet Muhammad ﷺ was sent with three aims; firstly, to recite to the Sahābah ؓ the Noble Qur'ān; secondly, to teach them the Noble Qur'ān and the Ahādeeth (the scholars have said that 'wisdom' in this context means the Noble Ahādeeth) and finally, Allāh ﷻ gave the order of purifying them (Islāh). The Noble Prophet Muhammad ﷺ alone carried out all 3 of these, however, today they have all been split up and shared; different scholars have chosen their respective fields, so it is up to us to approach the scholars. The Maktab system was set up so the recitation could be taught. The Dārul-Ulooms were set up so that the Noble Qur'ān and Noble Ahādeeth could be taught. But why has everybody forgotten about the spiritual retreats (known as Khānqah or Zāwiyah) which were set up so that spiritual rectification could be taught?

The Shaykh
In Tasawwuf, the Shaykh has the same role as a Mufassir in Tafseer or a Muhaddith in Hadeeth. Many people may deny the need of a Shaykh. However, in this day and age, it is extremely vital that every single one of us finds a true Shaykh who will help us travel the path of Tasawwuf and help us become a pious friend of Allāh ﷻ.

Shaykh Maseehullāh Khān Sāhib ؒ has written the following in his book, The Path to Perfection, "It has always been the Divine scheme of things that perfection cannot be attained without an experienced instructor (Ustādh). Thus, when one is endowed with the guidance to enter into the path, one should search for an instructor of the path."

It is from the great wisdom of Allāh ﷻ that He sent the Noble Prophet Muhammad ﷺ to represent the need of a Shaykh. Allāh ﷻ could have, by all means, sent the Noble Qur'ān and Noble Ahādeeth without the Holy Prophet ﷺ but He wanted to show that nobody can become an expert without an expert teacher.

A note to the Students of Arabic: Shaykh Ashraf Alī Thānwī ﷺ was once approached by an Ālim, arguing that there is no need for a spiritual Shaykh. Hadhrat asked him, "In the Noble Qur'ān, is it correct where Allāh ﷻ has said وَيُزَكِّيهِمْ?" The Ālim replied in the affirmative. Hadhrat then asked, "Is يُزَكِّيهِمْ a Fe'il Lāzim or Fe'il Muta'addi?" The Ālim, at once, apologised and understood his mistake.

Another evidence from the Noble Qur'ān for the need of a Shaykh is the verse,

يَٰٓأَيُّهَا ٱلَّذِينَ ءَامَنُوا۟ ٱتَّقُوا۟ ٱللَّهَ وَكُونُوا۟ مَعَ ٱلصَّٰدِقِينَ

"O you who believe! Fear Allāh and be with those who are true (in words and deeds)." (9:119)

Those who read the Noble Qur'ān regularly will be aware of how often Allāh ﷻ says, "Fear Allāh" to the extent it is mentioned every 2nd or 3rd page but we rarely focus on this. I would therefore advise, every sincere seeker to first learn the basics of Tasawwuf and then find a true expert Shaykh who has achieved excellence at the hands of another. A true Shaykh is similar to a Muhaddith; they possess a spiritual chain and connection to the Noble Prophet Muhammad ﷺ (which is known as Silsilah). Justice to the topic of Tasawwuf has not been served, therefore an excellent book I would recommend all to study is 'The Path to Perfection' by Shaykh Maseehullāh Khān Sāhib ﷫.

May Allāh ﷻ accept this short article for His sake, accept me for the work of His Deen and may Allāh ﷻ accept the efforts of Shaykh Mufti Saiful Islām. Āmeen! (Hanzalah– JKN Student)

Memory of the Beloved Prophet ﷺ

Year 570 CE you were born in the Holy City of Makkah,
Wherein lies the beauty built by Sayyidunā Ibrāheem ﷷ and Ismāeel ﷷ, the exalted Ka'bah.

It had been 600 years since Sayyidunā Eesā ﷷ, this period also known in the Qur'an as 'Fatrah'.
You came at a time when the world was in darkness, people were lost, misguided and swimming in ignorance.
How auspicious that moment was for us all,
When beloved Āminah conceived and gave birth to such a blessed soul.

The world was illuminated brightly and the 1000 year old fire was extinguished suddenly.

The extravagant castles of Shām could be seen, oh, what a time this must have been.

The shadow of your father, the honourable Abdullāh, had already left this world.

This was just the start of your hardships, through which you were tumbled and turned.

It was at the tender age of six, your mother's gentle touch was no longer felt,
Heart wrenching, heart breaking, heart left to melt.

Then came along the dignified Abdul Muttalib who took you into his care,
O' Muhammad! Such an upbringing of pain and grief is seldom and very rare.

But Allāh gives the most difficult of battles to those,
Who are selected by Him and for His mission are chose.
After a year or two, Abdul Muttalib met his Lord – ache upon ache.
Such pain left you lonely and full of tears,

But this was part of Allāh's plan; to make you strong and without fears.

Now you stayed with your uncle, an orphan, aged eight,
Abū Tālib was his name, he loved you and the affection he showed was great.

You herded sheep and became a shepherd,
You became known for truthfulness and honesty, a man of his word.

You later grew into a fine man and started to trade,
Which attracted the attention of Sayyidah Khadeejah whose husband you were later made.

You lived happily and had six children,
Four blessed daughters; two beloved sons (who died as infants).
Zaynab, Ruqayyah, Umm Kulthoom, Fātimah,

Little Qāsim and how can we forget Abdullāh?
As time went by, and evil began to spread,
A lot of thoughts started going through your head.

You looked at people, as they worshipped idols carved from their own hands,
And over trivial issues, how a clan would fight with other clans.

The people of Arabia mercilessly buried their baby daughters alive,
And they did not ever fulfil the rights of their children and wives.
People deprived the poor and didn't give the weak their rights,

Men merrily drank wine and gambled throughout the night.

Shedding blood and killing was prevalent,
The sanctity of human life had become totally irrelevant.

Little did they know how their lives were about to be turned,
As the light of Prophethood shone, glimmering bright, like a lantern you burned.

One day, in Mount Hira as you were meditating,
An angel descended and started communicating.

"Read! O Muhammad, Read!" Were the first words said,
You were scared and frightened and quickly rushed ahead.

Upon reaching home, sweating and panicking you screamed,
"O Khadeejah! Wrap me quick!" a large blanket, warm and thick.

Alarmed, petrified and terrified, as any wife would be,
She obeyed instantly, as she was the first believer (in Islām).

"Fear not! O Muhammad" She said. "In your Lord we trust and you must not despair.
You join ties with relatives, ease people's burdens and treat your guests with utmost care."

Your mission had now started; Islām was universal, for one and all.

The task was not an easy one; due to opposition, very few listened and heeded the call.

The very first believers were keen and true, Khadeejah, Abū Bakr, Zayd and Ali (your father's nephew).

But the call to One God was not happily welcomed or could be seen. Abū Tālib was told, "Tell Muhammad to renounce his Deen."

If they were to put the sun in your right hand and the moon in your left, you would not have given up.
Whether it meant you were tortured, beaten or accused of being corrupt.

It was such a shame; they titled you as a magician and poet instead of your beloved name.
"He's a soothsayer," did they claim. For causing disunity, only you did they blame.

You taught the purpose of life; life is not a game.
"I call you to One God; like all Messengers, without any wage nor fame."

After ten years of Prophethood, you lost two Companions, loyal and faithful.
They would always be joint at your hip; the first was your uncle Abū Tālib.

Then Sayyidah Khadeejah your wife, who would have for you,
even sacrificed her life.

Then one dark night, Angel Jib'reel ﷺ descended.
He took you on a long journey which was blessed and splendid.

From the sacred house in Makkah all the way to Jerusalem, then to the seven heavens and high above.
You travelled on the Burāq with speed, flying high like a dove.

The very same night you returned home safe, to Makkah.
With a gift from your Lord, to the believers, it was the Salāh.

Now the time came to migrate to Madeenah.
And it wasn't long before the first battle, Badr, took place in the 2nd year of Hijrah.

The enemy was strong, 1000 men fully equipped to their teeth.
The Muslims were less, actually very few, but they were neither disheartened nor felt blue.

This was a lesson in history, to be recorded.
Even if you are few, but sincerely true, Allāh's ﷻ help arrives and you will be rewarded.

The help of Allāh ﷻ came and flocks of angels over the blue skies flew.
Supporting the believers, who were devoted and close to you.

Although ill-equipped, weak and poor, Muslims were granted victory. This was a day celebrated and remembered in history!

5 Ways to Make your Child Love to Pray

Like some mothers out there, ever since my baby turned 'the big 7', I've struggled on how to encourage him to pray consistently. I say the big 7 as a joke, because we all know they're not so grown-up, actually quite far from it. However, we are well aware that this is the age we need to get a bit serious and encourage our kids to begin good, wholesome habits. And what better habit is there than our five daily prayers? Here are some things to think about when encouraging this wonderful habit:

1. Make Prayer a Priority for Yourself First
When I think back at my childhood, I remember one sweet memory which has connected me to prayer today. It is seeing my dad sitting peacefully in prayer every morning and every evening. I would stand there in awe, watching him from a distance, absorbing the peace and enjoying the beauty, Subhān-Allāh.

No matter where you are, if you're outside or on the road, when you realise its prayer time, pull over and let your kids see you keep your prayer. Of course, choose a spot where you feel comfortable and safe, but don't demand that your child pray. Focus on yourself. Rush to pray and speak aloud saying something like, "Subhān-

Allāh, I need to pray asap, Allāh ﷻ is waiting for me!"

What does this display to your child?
You're showing them your desire to please Allāh ﷻ, your need to thank your Lord, your passion to keep a promise to perform an obligatory act, and your deep commitment to connect with the Creator, Who is in charge of everything! Your willingness to stop what you are doing in order to pray, is totally crucial, especially when little wondering eyes are watching. So go on, walk the walk and ease-up on talking the talk. There's much wisdom in this.

2. Be Happy and Display Warmth When Reminding Your Child to Pray
In the morning, when you wake up for Fajr, give yourself enough time to pray slowly and recite the Qur'ān for a good amount of time, enough time for it to comfort your heart and soul. It's different for everyone. I personally prefer reciting certain Sūrah's of the Qur'ān.

Once you've received your dose of energy, only then are you in the right frame of mind to remind your child of their obligation to pray Fajr. How do you wake them up? Definitely not by yelling or banging on their door with a demanding tone. In my home, our rule is 'no locking bedroom doors', but we've formed a habit of knocking and waiting for permission before entering a room, even if the door is wide open. It's from a Hadeeth of our blessed Prophet ﷺ. I knock on their door gently and say, "Assalāmu Alaikum my sweethearts. Rise and shine, it's Fajr time!" Then I sit at the end of their bed, and recite in my most comforting voice, a Sūrah which I love. If it is short, I just keep repeating it a few times, slowly allowing it to penetrate deep into my inner soul. It helps when I close my eyes. Alternatively, I will play the Qur'ān on my phone, or read Du'ās from a book. You can also use this time to teach your kids and yourself, the Du'ā that is recited upon rising from sleep.

In either case, I'm using the beautiful words of Allāh ﷻ, to carry my children from their phase of slumber to wakefulness. There are immense blessings in these words, which can bring ease to any difficult situation, especially a hard sleep. Try it, you'll be quite surprised. My children appreciate this gentle nudge so much, that they peek their little heads from under their covers within minutes and say, "Assalāmu Alaikum mummy! I'm awake, I'm awake!" and willingly go on to their morning routine. No yelling, no pulling and no stressful start for anyone, only good memories!

3. Draw a Beautiful Picture of Prayer
Children love to hear a story which will forever paint a lovely picture in their mind. We should use stories as an alternative in teaching them something important, so that it can have a deep and meaningful impact on their lives. The Prophet Yaqūb ﷺ used to tell his son Sayyidunā Yūsuf ﷺ stories in the most beautiful description. Many of us have not been given this gift by our parents. Instead, we have been told that we must pray and if we do not, we will be punished. Let's avoid connecting prayer with punishment when addressing it with our children. Instead, describe to them the immense love that

Allāh ﷻ has for them. The love and beauty that can be found in prayer. Begin with explaining to your child what prayer means to you.

How many prayers and at what age?

I'm sure we've all struggled with this idea. We listen to a lecture, or read about the Fiqh rulings on prayer and wonder, 'What should I expect from my child or young adult?' We've gone as far as telling our 7, 8 or 9-year-old, that they must pray 5 times a day or else! I have done it and later felt terrible about it because the outcome was not positive and my approach was all wrong. Let's first look at what our goals and challenges are:

Our Goals

- We want our child to form a habit of praying.
- We want our child to love to speak to their Lord.
- We want to implement in our child a desire to pray.
- We want our child to understand that it's an obligation and not a choice.

Our Struggles

- Some of us have a few years of missed prayers, and find it a struggle to make them up. We do not want our child to go through this.
- We do not want our child to hate the idea of prayer or to attribute it to something negative.
- We don't want our child to lie about praying or say they prayed but did not perform the action.

Think about yourself and your ups and downs during the year and be very honest with yourself. Throughout the 12 months, are you super-duper punctual and focused in every single prayer? Or are you an ordinary person struggling, but slowly improving by the years. You have your good days and your slip-ups. So how can we expect our children to be perfect? Our Merciful Lord knows that we are human and we will make mistakes. Allāh ﷻ loves to forgive us. He has set up a designated special time to ask for forgiveness, every single night after Ishā. Let us focus on what is important when it comes to prayer, i.e. to improve slowly, but consistently throughout our life.

4. Be Gentle and Patient When it Comes to Prayer

I know there are Fiqh rules and obligations to prayer which we must follow. I also know that habits take long to form. Teaching your kids to pray at an early age is a great idea. The best way to implement a rule or to follow a law, is to be strict on yourself and patient and forgiving on others around you.

When it's time to pray,

- Remind your child in a pleasant way.
- Ask your son if he'd like to perform the Adhān and call everyone to prayer.
- Encourage your children to pray in congregation with one another to get more reward.
- Perform your prayer in front of your children, whether they join in or not. Then leave it at that.

5. If Your Child Prays, Praise and Make Du'ā for Them Out Loud
A few things I say to my kids when they pray are,
- "Māshā-Allāh, may Allāh ﷻ reward you. You look so beautiful when you pray. May Allāh ﷻ fill your face with Noor (light), Āmeen."
- "Subhān-Allāh, did you all see how lovely she performed her prayer, may Allah ﷻ always protect and guide you my sweet, Āmeen."
- "Alhamdulillāh, you make me so happy when you do things that are pleasing to Allāh ﷻ. May He always guide you to do that which is pleasing to Him, Āmeen."

Kissing or hugging your child, is another wonderful way to show your love and approval of them. A few years ago, I was very strict when it came to implementing prayer on my child. I would remind him over and over and pick on what he did incorrectly when it came to the steps of prayer. I thought this was my duty, but I quickly realised it was doing more harm. So I stopped when I realised my error. It is never too late to change your way and attitude. Now I follow these 5 steps and over time, I have seen a change in how my son sees prayer, Alhamdulillāh!

Here is an example. The other day, we were on our way to a swimming class for my kids and were short on time. I had performed my prayer, but they hadn't. While driving to their class, I asked them if they had prayed and one of my kids exclaimed, "Oh mummy, I forgot"! My oldest child chipped in and said, "You know what? We can pray in the dressing room after the swimming class when we take a shower, we will be clean and ready." I smiled and said, "Māshā-Allāh! Thank you Abdullāh, that's a great idea!"

Alhamdulillāh, I thought, hand on my heart and feeling so good, patience, time and gentleness really do pay off! O', Allāh ﷻ please give us the patience to guide our children on the road which is most pleasing to You, Āmeen!

Rise Among the Elite

You just know your day is going to be so good when you have done this particular prayer. It brings so much difference, Allāhu-Akbar!

How great it is to wake up with an intention of worshipping Allāh ﷻ, with thanking Him for the Mercy He has given, that you are about to live another day and for the opportunity to say Alhamdulillāh, Subhān-Allāh or recite Durood Shareef. When a person enters Jannah, they will regret that they did not spend more time praising the Almighty. These are just the little things that we do not seem to give so much attention to in our daily lives, yet these little things are the ones who bear so much Ajr (reward)

Have we even noticed that in the word Fajr the Arabic term for reward [Ajr] is present too?

During my advertising class at college, we have this thing called branding sessions. It is the part of the lecture wherein the professor is to brand you. It is more like make your name sweet and stand out. It is a beautiful way of uplifting the confidence of a person to the point that he or she would deliver his or her work in a manner that no arrogance will take over but excellence would be present.

Now, this is how I always felt about Fajr. It gives the Muslims a 'branding' in that sense. It makes a Muslim stand out from all his/her works, again not in arrogance but because that person knows well from whom He came, what his/her purpose is and of course, to Whom he/she will return. Hence, his/her works and Ibādah are aimed to be done in excellence.

Fajr always reminds me of the Sahābah ﷺ and for countless times, I always find myself thinking about them and imagining how it would feel if I was among them. They would worship Allāh ﷻ in such a beautiful way before and after Fajr, unfortunately, unlike most of the Ummah today who are enjoying their sleep at this time.

I know there are a lot of stories amongst them that will inspire us, but to me, I would always remember the story of Sayyidah Umme Waraqah ﷺ. Some may find it weird but it's actually the story of her death that I always remember during Fajr, but it is really motivating when we remember death as often as we could.

This woman was attached to the Holy Qur'ān to the extent that she would recite it every day and night and even at the time of her death, it was that very Qur'ān which made Sayyidunā Umar ﷺ notice that something was not right because he did not hear Sayyidah Umm Waraqah ﷺ reciting the Holy Qur'ān from her house that Fajr morning of her death.

Subhān-Allāh. How wonderful is this person! It must have been her daily deed to recite and put herself in Dhikr, exalting Allāh ﷻ.

And how many of us even give enough time to recite or read the Holy Qur'ān after we wake up or even before we sleep?

Let us rise among the elite. Rise among those who gain such beautiful Ajr!

Remember the beautiful reward that Fajr brings, as said by the Holy Prophet ﷺ, "He who performs the dawn prayer will be under the protection of Allāh ﷻ." (Muslim)

What harm can come to you when it is Allāh ﷻ that protects you? Allāhu-Akbar! And we pray that Allāh ﷻ makes us among those very people who would wake up with the beautiful intention of worshipping, thanking and asking for His Forgiveness. Āmeen!

The Woman Who was Given the Title 'The Martyr' Whilst She was Living!

The tittle was given by no other than the Messenger of Allāh ﷺ. Along with the great Sahābah ؓ, who would only address her with this title, 'The Martyr'.

When she tried to ask permission from the Holy Prophet ﷺ to go and join the Battle of Badr with the intention to nurse and help out with medical attention, the Holy Prophet ﷺ declined and told her, "Stay in your house, Allāh ﷻ will bless you with martyrdom."

Do you have any clue now, who this blessed woman was? Yes, I am talking about Sayyidah Umm Waraqah ؓ, the woman who devoted all her life in increasing her closeness to Allāh ﷻ through living and dedicating herself with the Qur'ān.

By Allāh ﷻ, this woman devoted her attention to the Noble Qur'ān. Through reading it, memorising it and following its teachings and rules, she made it her main concern in all aspects of her private and public life and through the Qur'ān, she also attained a high and noble status.

Sayyidah Umm Waraqah ؓ was one of the earliest Ansāri female Companion that entered the fold of Islām. She was of high and noble lineage and indeed, she was a very wealthy woman, but her luxuries in life did not shun her from devoting herself solely to things that would bring her close to Allāh ﷻ.

After the incident of her asking the Holy Prophet ﷺ to allow her to go for Jihād and was declined, she believed and obeyed.

One day, she asked for a Mu'addhin for her house and the Holy Prophet ﷺ gave her one. She allocated a section of her big house as a praying area and she would make this place a place for Halaqa (study circle). She would lead in prayers some Muslim women of her family or whomsoever who came to meet her in her house.

Sayyidah Umm Waraqah ؓ was not married despite her nobility, wealth and everything she had, for she was deeply influenced by the picture of the bliss of Paradise that never changes or comes to an end. She had one housemaid and one male servant who served her in her big house, but these two were not treated differently to her; she treated them like a mother would treat her children.

She used to sleep very little in the night despite her old age and in hours of darkness, she would seek Allāh's ﷻ forgiveness and worship Him in humility. Every night she would pray and recite the Qur'ān abundantly.

One night, a caller called, "Come to martyrdom, O' Umm Waraqah! The time has come and your appointment with death is here! The earth is confined for you in spite of its vastness! What is with Allāh ﷻ is best and lasting! You certainly have nearness to Allāh ﷻ and a good place of return!"

On that very night, her servant and the maid stood up and strangled Sayyidah Umm Waraqah ؓ to death. They then wrapped her in a piece of cloth and put her at a side of the house and fled.

Sayyidunā Umar ؓ, who was the Ameerul Mu'mineen of that time, woke up for Fajr and observed something that attracted his attention. When he finished praying, he went out and told the people, "By Allāh ﷻ I did not hear the recitation of my Umm Waraqah ؓ last night!"

It was for this reason that he came to her house in the company of some other Sahābah ؓ to see what had happened to Sayyidah Umm

Waraqah ﷺ. When they entered, they found no one and they did not hear any movement. It was then that Sayyidunā Umar ؓ sensed that something had happened to her!

Suddenly, they found her wrapped in a piece of cloth, dead. Sayyidunā Umar ؓ then said, "Allāh ﷻ and His Messenger ﷺ spoke the truth!" Those who were with him also echoed, "Allāh ﷻ and His Messenger ﷺ spoke the truth!"

Subhān-Allāh! Did she die in vain? No, she did not! For Paradise was her abode! What a beautiful and inspiring woman Sayyidah Umm Waraqah ؓ was!

We pray to Allāh ﷻ that He accepts her and raises her status in Jannah! Āmeen!

There are many beautiful points to consider in this story; her love for Allāh ﷻ, her obedience towards the Messenger of Allāh ﷺ, her devotion to the Qur'ān, her Da'wah to other women and her kind treatment to her servants.

Her devotion to the Qur'ān was of great dedication. Imagine, Sayyidunā Umar ؓ noticed immediately something wrong when he did not hear the recitation of Sayyidah Umm Waraqah ؓ! So realise that she had been consistently reciting every night, when some of us cannot even stand to listen to three minutes of recitation of the Qur'ān! My brothers and sisters in Islām, these are the kind of people that we should be inspired by; people we should take our Deen from. Martyrdom is not just about going to battles, for we ourselves are already in Jihād with our Nafs.

I ask you all, to please mention the name of Sayyidah Umm Waraqah in your Duās in your next Salāh. May Allāh ﷻ be truly pleased with her. Āmeen!

A Glimpse into the Nurturing of Maulāna As'ad Madani ؓ of his Daughter

The following lines are a selected translation of a biography of Ameer-ul-Hind Maulāna Sayyid As'ad Madani ؓ, written by his eldest daughter, in which she explains how her noble father saw to her upbringing, how he would conduct himself with his children and how he would spare no efforts in seeing to their needs and keeping them happy.

He undertook the burden of seeing to the needs of not only the nation, but nevertheless he still found the time to fulfil the rights of his family as well. At the end, it includes some advices Maulānā As'ad ؓ gave to his daughter in a letter after her marriage was solemnised. Indeed, the advices in this letter are so valuable that it would be most appropriate if it could be framed and given to every newly-married girl to hang in her house and reflect on daily.

The daughter writes:

1) What can I say regarding the favours he showered upon me! If his love, compassion and sacrifice for strangers knew no limits, then what would you expect his conduct with his daughter to be!

2) My beloved father paid great attention to my nurturing. He taught me the laws of Salāh, Sawm, Zakāh and Hajj; how to entertain guests, look after ones home; importance of modesty and the veil.
In short, my father played a vital role in every aspect of my life. From an early age, he instilled within us the importance of Salāh. Even on journeys, he would never allow us to delay our Salāh. He himself would stand with us behind a covering and pour water for us. It is for this reason that, delaying Salāh has become practically impossible for us.

3) He instilled within our hearts the love of fasting as well while we were still very young. Every year, on the day of Eid, he would ask us how many fasts we had kept and for every fast he would give us a rupee.

4) He himself taught me the etiquettes of entertaining guests, of talking and even how to cook. He would sit with me in the kitchen and show me how to make various dishes. For this reason, today, I find no greater enjoyment than what I find in the kitchen.
5) Whenever I would fall ill, especially during pregnancy my father would call my home immediately. He would personally see to all my medical needs and expenses. After getting married, my father sent me the following letter:

$$\text{بِسْمِ اللّٰهِ الرَّحْمٰنِ الرَّحِيْمِ}$$

My beloved daughter! May Allāh ﷻ keep you happy in this world as well as in the next. O my daughter! This world will only last for a few days. Thus, it would indeed be most foolish if one were to destroy his ever-lasting abode in its pursuit. From now on you are responsible for your own life.

We have become old and ones parents cannot remain with one forever. Thus, before doing anything, ponder over its benefits and harms. Those who love you understand well the advantages and disadvantages of what you wish to do and Allāh ﷻ is the One Who loves you the most and understands you the best (thus, always follow His commands).

Your family inheritance was never a criteria, nor kinship; rather, it is piety and connection with Allāh ﷻ. Thus if you suffer a setback in Dunya (wealth etc.), you have not lost a great deal.

You are now going to a new family. Every action and word of yours will be scrutinised.

Regarding clothing, shun fashion and blind imitation, rather let modesty and piety guide you in choosing your clothing.

Avoid mingling with others excessively. Talking less and mixing less has always saved one from difficulties. Associate only with those whom your seniors are pleased with. Always present yourself in front of others with a smiling face, good character and humility. Regard yourself as the most inferior, no matter how evil others appear to be. If you take your in-laws as your seniors and regard them to be your well wishers, you shall never be disgraced.

Before marriage, after Allāh ﷻ and the Holy Prophet ﷺ, the rank of your mother and father was the highest. However, now after marriage, the rank of the husband takes third place (i.e. above your parents as well). Never act against his wishes.

If you do your own work whilst serving others, all shall respect you. If you prefer luxury, rest and taking work from others, you will drop in the eyes of all. Take care of the items in your house as well. Do not allow anything to get lost. Keep everything clean and in its place. After using anything stored in bottles, ensure that their lids are closed properly. Place them in the same spot you took them from. Have set places for all items, clothing etc., so that you may find it whenever you need it.

Instill within yourself the habit of performing Salāh at its fixed times, with proper devotion and concentration.

Ungratefulness and backbiting are the worst habits of women. Avoid them completely.

(Ameerul-Hind) Maulāna As'ad ؒ

Other titles from JKN Publications

Your Questions Answered
An outstanding book written by Shaykh Mufti Saiful Islām. A very comprehensive yet simple Fatāwa book and a source of guidance that reaches out to a wider audience i.e. the English speaking Muslims. The reader will benefit from the various answers to questions based on the Laws of Islām relating to the beliefs of Islām, knowledge, Sunnah, pillars of Islām, marriage, divorce and contemporary issues.

UK RRP: £7.50

Hadeeth for Beginners
A concise Hadeeth book with various Ahādeeth that relate to basic Ibādāh and moral etiquettes in Islām accessible to a wider readership. Each Hadeeth has been presented with the Arabic text, its translation and commentary to enlighten the reader, its meaning and application in day-to-day life.

UK RRP: £3.00

Du'ā for Beginners
This book contains basic Du'ās which every Muslim should recite on a daily basis. Highly recommended to young children and adults studying at Islamic schools and Madrasahs so that one may cherish the beautiful treasure of supplications of our beloved Prophet ﷺ in one's daily life, which will ultimately bring peace and happiness in both worlds, Inshā-Allāh.

UK RRP: £2.00

How well do you know Islām?
An exciting educational book which contains 300 multiple questions and answers to help you increase your knowledge on Islām! Ideal for the whole family, especially children and adult students to learn new knowledge in an enjoyable way and cherish the treasures of knowledge that you will acquire from this book. A very beneficial tool for educational syllabus.

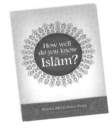

UK RRP: £3.00

Treasures of the Holy Qur'ān
This book entitled "Treasures of the Holy Qur'ān" has been compiled to create a stronger bond between the Holy Qur'ān and the readers. It mentions the different virtues of Sūrahs and verses from the Holy Qur'ān with the hope that the readers will increase their zeal and enthusiasm to recite and inculcate the teachings of the Holy Qur'ān into their daily lives.

UK RRP: £3.00

Other titles from JKN PUBLICATIONS

Marriage - A Complete Solution
Islām regards marriage as a great act of worship. This book has been designed to provide the fundamental teachings and guidelines of all what relates to the marital life in a simplified English language. It encapsulates in a nutshell all the marriage laws mentioned in many of the main reference books in order to facilitate their understanding and implementation.

UK RRP: £5.00

Pearls of Luqmān
This book is a comprehensive commentary of Sūrah Luqmān, written beautifully by Shaykh Mufti Saiful Islām. It offers the reader with an enquiring mind, abundance of advice, guidance, counselling and wisdom.

The reader will be enlightened by many wonderful topics and anecdotes mentioned in this book, which will create a greater understanding of the Holy Qur'ān and its wisdom. The book highlights some of the wise sayings and words of advice Luqmān gave to his son.

Arabic Grammar for Beginners
This book is a study of Arabic Grammar based on the subject of Nahw (Syntax) in a simplified English format. If a student studies this book thoroughly, he/she will develop a very good foundation in this field, Inshā-Allāh. Many books have been written on this subject in various languages such as Arabic, Persian and Urdu. However, in this day and age there is a growing demand for this subject to be available in English.

UK RRP: £3.00

A Gift to My Youngsters
This treasure filled book, is a collection of Islamic stories, morals and anecdotes from the life of our beloved Prophet ﷺ, his Companions and the pious predecessors. The stories and anecdotes are based on moral and ethical values, which the reader will enjoy sharing with their peers, friends, families and loved ones.

"A Gift to My Youngsters" – is a wonderful gift presented to the readers personally, by the author himself, especially with the youngsters in mind. He has carefully selected stories and anecdotes containing beautiful morals, lessons and valuable knowledge and wisdom.

UK RRP: £5.00

Travel Companion
The beauty of this book is that it enables a person on any journey, small or distant or simply at home, to utilise their spare time to read and benefit from an exciting and vast collection of important and interesting Islamic topics and lessons. Written in simple and easy to read text, this book will immensely benefit both the newly interested person in Islām and the inquiring mind of a student expanding upon their existing knowledge. Inspiring reminders from the Holy Qur'ān and the blessed words of our beloved Prophet ﷺ beautifies each topic and will illuminate the heart of the reader.
UK RRP: £5.00

Pearls of Wisdom
Junaid Baghdādi ﷺ once said, "Allāh ﷻ strengthens through these Islamic stories the hearts of His friends, as proven from the Qur'anic verse,
"And all that We narrate unto you of the stories of the Messengers, so as to strengthen through it your heart." (11:120)
Mālik Ibn Dinār ﷺ stated that such stories are gifts from Paradise. He also emphasised to narrate these stories as much as possible as they are gems and it is possible that an individual might find a truly rare and invaluable gem among them.
UK RRP: £6.00

Inspirations
This book contains a compilation of selected speeches delivered by Shaykh Mufti Saiful Islām on a variety of topics such as the Holy Qur'ān, Nikāh and eating Halāl. Having previously been compiled in separate booklets, it was decided that the transcripts be gathered together in one book for the benefit of the reader. In addition to this, we have included in this book, further speeches which have not yet been printed.
UK RRP: £6.00

Gift to my Sisters
A thought provoking compilation of very interesting articles including real life stories of pious predecessors, imaginative illustrations and much more. All designed to influence and motivate mothers, sisters, wives and daughters towards an ideal Islamic lifestyle. A lifestyle referred to by our Creator, Allāh ﷻ in the Holy Qur'ān as the means to salvation and ultimate success.
UK RRP: £6.00

Gift to my Brothers
A thought provoking compilation of very interesting articles including real life stories of pious predecessors, imaginative illustrations, medical advices on intoxicants and rehabilitation and much more. All designed to influence and motivate fathers, brothers, husbands and sons towards an ideal Islamic lifestyle. A lifestyle referred to by our Creator, Allāh ﷻ in the Holy Qur'ān as the means to salvation and ultimate success.
UK RRP: £5.00

Heroes of Islām

"In the narratives there is certainly a lesson for people of intelligence (understanding)." (12:111)
A fine blend of Islamic personalities who have been recognised for leaving a lasting mark in the hearts and minds of people.
A distinguishing feature of this book is that the author has selected not only some of the most world and historically famous renowned scholars but also these lesser known and a few who have simply left behind a valuable piece of advice to their nearest and dearest.
UK RRP: £5.00

Ask a Mufti (3 volumes)

Muslims in every generation have confronted different kinds of challenges. Inspite of that, Islām produced such luminary Ulamā who confronted and responded to the challenges of their time to guide the Ummah to the straight path.
"Ask A Mufti" is a comprehensive three volume fatwa book, based on the Hanafi School, covering a wide range of topics related to every aspect of human life such as belief, ritual worship, life after death and contemporary legal topics related to purity, commercial transaction, marriage, divorce, food, cosmetic, laws pertaining to women, Islamic medical ethics and much more.
UK RRP: £30.00

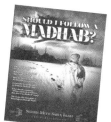

Should I Follow a Madhab?

Taqleed or following one of the four legal schools is not a new phenomenon. Historically, scholars of great calibre and luminaries, each one being a specialist in his own right, were known to have adhered to one of the four legal schools. It is only in the previous century that a minority group emerged advocating a severe ban on following one of the four major schools.
This book endeavours to address the topic of Taqleed and elucidates its importance and necessity in this day and age. It will also, by the Divine Will of Allāh dispel some of the confusion surrounding this topic.
UK RRP: £5.00

Advice for the Students of Knowledge

Allāh ﷻ describes divine knowledge in the Holy Qur'ān as a 'Light'. Amongst the qualities of light are purity and guidance. The Holy Prophet ﷺ has clearly explained this concept in many blessed Ahādeeth and has also taught us many supplications in which we ask for beneficial knowledge.
This book is a golden tool for every sincere student of knowledge wishing to mould his/her character and engrain those correct qualities in order to be worthy of receiving the great gift of Ilm from Allāh ﷻ.
UK RRP: £3.00

Stories for Children

"Stories for Children" - is a wonderful gift presented to the readers personally by the author himself, especially with the young children in mind. The stories are based on moral and ethical values, which the reader will enjoy sharing with their peers, friends, families and loved ones. The aim is to present to the children stories and incidents which contain moral lessons, in order to reform and correct their lives, according to the Holy Qur'ān and Sunnah.
UK RRP: £5.00

Pearls from My Shaykh
This book contains a collection of pearls and inspirational accounts of the Holy Prophet ﷺ, his noble Companions, pious predecessors and some personal accounts and sayings of our well-known contemporary scholar and spiritual guide, Shaykh Mufti Saiful Islām Sāhib. Each anecdote and narrative of the pious predecessors have been written in the way that was narrated by Mufti Saiful Islām Sāhib in his discourses, drawing the specific lessons he intended from telling the story. The accounts from the life of the Shaykh has been compiled by a particular student based on their own experience and personal observation. **UK RRP: £5.00**

Paradise & Hell
This book is a collection of detailed explanation of Paradise and Hell including the state and conditions of its inhabitants. All the details have been taken from various reliable sources. The purpose of its compilation is for the reader to contemplate and appreciate the innumerable favours, rewards, comfort and unlimited luxuries of Paradise and at the same time take heed from the punishment of Hell. Shaykh Mufti Saiful Islām Sāhib has presented this book in a unique format by including the Tafseer and virtues of Sūrah Ar-Rahmān. **UK RRP: £5.00**

Prayers for Forgiveness
Prayers for Forgiveness' is a short compilation of Du'ās in Arabic with English translation and transliteration. This book can be studied after 'Du'ā for Beginners' or as a separate book. It includes twenty more Du'ās which have not been mentioned in the previous Du'ā book. It also includes a section of Du'ās from the Holy Qur'ān and a section from the Ahādeeth. The book concludes with a section mentioning the Ninety-Nine Names of Allāh ﷻ with its translation and transliteration. **UK RRP: £3.00**

Scattered Pearls
This book is a collection of scattered pearls taken from books, magazines, emails and WhatsApp messages. These pearls will hopefully increase our knowledge, wisdom and make us realise the purpose of life. In this book, Mufti Sāhib has included messages sent to him from scholars, friends and colleagues which will be beneficial and interesting for our readers Inshā-Allāh. **UK RRP: £4.00**

Poems of Wisdom
This book is a collection of poems from those who contributed to the Al-Mumin Magazine in the poems section. The Hadeeth mentions "Indeed some form of poems are full of wisdom." The themes of each poem vary between wittiness, thought provocation, moral lessons, emotional to name but a few. The readers will benefit from this immensely and make them ponder over the outlook of life in general.
UK RRP: £4.00

This book is a detailed and informative commentary of the first three Sūrahs of the last Juz namely; Sūrah Naba, Sūrah Nāzi'āt and Sūrah Abasa. These Sūrahs vividly depict the horrific events and scenes of the Great Day in order to warn mankind the end of this world. These Sūrahs are an essential reminder for us all to instil the fear and concern of the Day of Judgement and to detach ourselves from the worldly pleasures. Reading this book allows us to attain the true realization of this world and provides essential advices of how to gain eternal salvation in the Hereafter.
RRP: £5:00

It is necessary that Muslims always strive to better themselves at all times and to free themselves from the destructive maladies. This book focusses on three main spiritual maladies; pride, anger and evil gazes. It explains its root causes and offers some spiritual cures. Many examples from the lives of the pious predecessors are used for inspiration and encouragement for controlling the above three maladies. It is hoped that the purification process of the heart becomes easy once the underlying roots of the above maladies are clearly understood.   **UK RRP: £5:00**

This book is a step by step guide on Hajj and Umrah for absolute beginners. Many other additional important rulings (Masāil) have been included that will Insha-Allāh prove very useful for our readers. The book also includes some etiquettes of visiting (Ziyārat) of the Holy Prophet's ﷺ blessed Masjid and his Holy Grave.
UK   RRP   £3:00

This book contains essential guidelines for a spiritual Mureed to gain some familiarity of the science of Tasawwuf. It explains the meaning and aims of Tasawwuf, some understanding around the concept of the soul, and general guidelines for a spiritual Mureed. This is highly recommended book and it is hoped that it gains wider readership among those Mureeds who are basically new to the science of Tasawwuf.
UK RRP £3:00

This book is a compilation of sayings and earnest pieces of advice that have been gathered directly from my respected teacher Shaykh Mufti Saiful Islām Sāhib. The book consists of many valuable enlightenments including how to deal with challenges of life, promoting unity, practicing good manners, being optimistic and many other valuable advices. Our respected Shaykh has gathered this Naseehah from meditating, contemplating, analysing and searching for the gems within Qur'anic verses, Ahādeeth and teachings of our Pious Predecessors. **UK RRP £1:00**